THE SCIENCE OF ASPECTS

Ruskin: Study of Rocks in the Pass of Killiecrankie, 1857

The Science of Aspects

The Changing Role of Fact in the Work of Coleridge, Ruskin and Hopkins

by

PATRICIA M. BALL

UNIVERSITY OF LONDON
THE ATHLONE PRESS
1971

Published by
THE ATHLONE PRESS
UNIVERSITY OF LONDON
at 2 Gower Street, London WC1

*Distributed by Tiptree Book Services Ltd
Tiptree, Essex*

*U.S.A.
Oxford University Press Inc
New York*

ISBN 0 485 11123 3

Printed in Great Britain by
WESTERN PRINTING SERVICES LTD
BRISTOL

for
J.E.B.

ACKNOWLEDGMENTS

I should like to thank Royal Holloway College for the sabbatical leave which gave me time to write this book. To Professor Barbara Hardy and all my colleagues in the English Department, who helped to make the leave possible, I am particularly indebted.

April 1970   P.M.B.

. . . there is a science of the aspects of things, as well as of their nature; and it is as much a fact to be noted in their constitution, that they produce such and such an effect upon the eye or heart . . . as that they are made up of certain atoms or vibrations of matter.

Modern Painters III, ch. xvii, §43

CONTENTS

Abbreviations   x

Introduction   1

1   Coleridge and the World of Sense   5
    Theory (5)
    Descriptive Prose (11)
    Poems (34)

2   Ruskin and 'The Pure Fact'   48
    Ruskin as Poet (48)
    The Pathetic Fallacy (59)
    Descriptive Prose (80)

3   Hopkins and 'The Sweet Especial Scene'   103
    Theory (103)
    Descriptive Prose (115)
    Poems (132)
    Appendix. An uncollected letter from Hopkins
       to *Nature* (148)

Bibliography   151

Notes   153

Index   161

Frontispiece. Ruskin: Study of Rocks in the Pass of Killiecrankie
    Reproduced by permission of the Syndics of the Fitzwilliam
    Museum, Cambridge

ABBREVIATIONS

For fuller details of the works listed here the reader is referred to the Bibliography

Cook	Cook, E. T., *The Life of John Ruskin*
Devlin	*The Sermons and Devotional Writings of Gerard Manley Hopkins*, ed. C. Devlin SJ
Diaries	*The Diaries of John Ruskin*, ed. J. Evans and J. H. Waterhouse
Dixon Corr.	*The Correspondence of Gerard Manley Hopkins and Richard Watson Dixon*, ed. C. C. Abbott
DWJ	*Journals of Dorothy Wordsworth*, ed. E. de Selincourt
Guide	Wordsworth, William, *A Guide through the District of the Lakes in the North of England*, ed. W. M. Merchant
JP	*The Journals and Papers of Gerard Manley Hopkins*, ed. H. House and G. Storey
Letters to Bridges	*The Letters of Gerard Manley Hopkins to Robert Bridges*, ed. C. C. Abbott
MP	Ruskin, John, *Modern Painters*
Notebooks	*The Notebooks of Samuel Taylor Coleridge*, ed. K. Coburn. References given indicate volume followed by entry number. The letter 'n' refers to volume containing editor's notes.
Shawcross	Coleridge, S. T., *Biographia Literaria and Aesthetical Essays*, ed. J. Shawcross
Works	*The Works of John Ruskin*, ed. E. T. Cook and A. Wedderburn

INTRODUCTION

THE COMMON ground which brings the names of Coleridge, Ruskin and Hopkins together in the first place is their passion for the natural world, and for recording their intense observation of it. Yet they react to this shared capacity for observation differently, interpret it differently, and evaluate it differently. Coleridge could say, in the course of working out his theory of imagination, that 'all objects (*as* objects) are essentially fixed and dead'; Ruskin opposes such a view fiercely, even while much that he says in *Modern Painters* about imagination is not remote from Coleridge's thought. If we read Hopkins's *The Starlight Night* with *Frost at Midnight*, we see great differences in the two poets' approach to the world around them. Hopkins's gaze is directed away from himself as he invites us to 'look, look up at the skies!'; Coleridge on the other hand relates the world to his own consciousness, rejoicing when he discovers in external things, 'dim sympathies with me who live'.

Even from this sketch of some of their contrasting reactions, we can begin to surmise that since the two Victorians both diverge from Coleridge we may well find their sympathies closer to each other. If, looking at the two poets, we feel that for all the bonds between them, the journey from one to the other has involved a change of centre or a shift of attitude, I would suggest that we need Ruskin to make more sense of such a process. Hopkins can be called 'a student of Ruskin'.[1] His poems can be seen as the outcome of a Romantic imagination worked upon and modified by Ruskin—a momentous development in nineteenth-century poetry and vision. In Hopkins, the clashes between Coleridge and Ruskin are seen to have been necessary for the renewal of poetic perception, and in him too, the opposition is reconciled with most fruitful results.

Ruskin's literary theories are as central as his descriptive writing to the tracing of these relationships. Particularly we have to think more positively about the pathetic fallacy than is customary now; as a phrase and as an idea, it is out of fashion and absent from current critical vocabularies. But a study of it reveals it to be a key symptom of the century's imaginative movements. As I hope to show, it leads us into larger issues, such as the relation of descriptive prose to the poetry of the century, and of Romantic to Ruskinian prose.

As the century goes on, there is 'a plainly developing literal vision'.[2] Qualities inherent in the object—shape, texture, structure—are of mounting importance. To the Romantics, 'the object had no significance in itself apart from the bestowal of, or explicit connection with, human passion';[3] to Ruskin in mid-century this connection was fallacious, and the object itself was the prize to be grasped as completely as possible by a concentrated study of its qualities—a study pointing on to what Hopkins implied in his term 'inscape'.

I want both to exhibit this change and to qualify it. Coleridge's Notebooks and other prose of the earlier period, such as Dorothy Wordsworth's journals, contrast with the poetic tendencies, in that the object is often vividly presented as itself and not merely as an appendage to human feeling. And on the Victorian side, the relation of poems to prose in Hopkins, and his whole vision, suggest qualifications to any theory of an absolute move in favour of the 'object in itself', which Ruskin may well seem to epitomize. Even in Ruskin's own writing, in his diaries and in *Modern Painters*, the relation between his literary theory and his practice in descriptive work yields more than a simple tendency towards appreciation of 'the pure fact'. He is both Romantic supporter and Romantic opponent, and out of the split his distinctive creative character is formed.

Other aspects of the topic are the two influences of science and the visual arts. Coleridge, Ruskin and Hopkins are all alert to the sciences of their day, and their imaginative work is conditioned by this interest, leading to interesting conjunctions of scientific and poetic awareness. Their emotional response to the world and their recognition of its features are both affected by the approach of botanist, geologist, meteorologist, or chemist, even though Ruskin is at pains to distinguish his 'science of aspects' from these other sciences.

Coleridge several times records his frustration at being unable to sketch what he sees; Ruskin and Hopkins were more fortunate, both being able draughtsmen. To all three, the keen visual sense of the painter is crucial, and here as with their scientific interests, their imaginative reaction to their environment is strengthened by their command of a specialized approach to forms and objects, as well as general powers of observation. Further, Ruskin's response to Turner is as central to his theories on imaginative power as Coleridge's admiration for Wordsworth: *Modern Painters* may be compared with *Biographia Literaria* in terms of their choice of hero. Both works celebrate and study the height of creative ability as it is found in a contemporary, but the change from the verbal to the visual genius is one of moment for the nineteenth-century mind. It symbolizes the growing prestige of objects and the growing obligation for the beholder to behold with full concentration, and with a regard for seeing as in itself a vital experience.

But exactly what is involved in such a development, and how far it is a move from Coleridge's position, we can only discover by closer examination of the various areas of thought and creative activity I have mentioned. I am suggesting that Coleridge, Ruskin and Hopkins form a reciprocal association, not a linear progression. In other words, I find the connections between them, the alliances and sympathies of vision, as substantial as the divergences and changes in point of view. The work of each illuminates that of the other two, and together they offer a pattern in which we can trace some of the imaginative features uniting and at the same time diversifying nineteenth-century writing.

3

COLERIDGE
AND THE WORLD OF SENSE

THEORY

As he works his way towards the definition of imagination in *Biographia Literaria* Coleridge establishes his fundamental philosophic principles with regard to the problem of man in relation to the universe around him. He first of all supports the commonsense approach which believes in an actual environment, the presence of a world 'out there' as reported by our senses. But our contact with that world and our awareness of it are not adequately explained by some theory of our passive dependence on physical stimuli from senses to brain, he maintains: 'all knowledge rests on the coincidence of an object with a subject', he says in Chapter XII,[1] and in the coinciding, the 'subject' is the active party. Perception is a creative act of mind making the object knowable; only by the initiative of the mind does the material world become accessible to us.

The context, therefore, for his theory of the essentially creative power of imagination is a general philosophy of the dominant force of the mind in the dealings between the self and the non-self. The poet's ability to quicken the materials he works with, to alchemize and unify them by his mental energies, is an intensified example of a power common to all of us in our daily recognition of our world: we make rather than observe what lies around us. And until, at the instigation of the self, some degree of fusion between subject and object has occurred, so that each has been impregnated with the other, even the world of rocks and stones and trees cannot exist for us, nor the ordinary relationships in this world of appearances. If the fusion occurs at the pitch of poetic imagination, then a universe of more profound relationships is revealed. So Coleridge arrives at the final part of his statement on imagination in Chapter XIII, where he summarizes his view of the relation between subject and object and clearly emphasizes his priorities in the last sentence on imagination itself: 'It is essentially *vital*, even as all objects (*as* objects) are essentially fixed and dead.'[2]

What he means by the vitalizing role of imagination, and how the poet's creativity differs from ordinary everyday perception, is illustrated in Chapter XV, where Shakespeare is considered as the type of poetic genius, exercising the powers of imagination in a consummate fashion. 'In this chapter', says Shawcross, 'we read that the mere faithful reproduction of natural appearances does not of itself mark the poet: that images drawn from nature become proofs of original genius only in respect of the transformation which they undergo under the action of the poetic spirit.' And the conclusion we are led to, he adds, is that 'the imagination . . . attains its highest potency when transfusing into the outward forms which it contemplates the emotional life which determines its activity'.[3] How Coleridge demonstrates these points is worth closer study.[4]

We do not become poets merely by seeing accurately and finding words which describe our observations faithfully. Copying the world of 'images' or objects will not take us beyond the elementary level of creativity, that which enables us to see what is before us without any recognition of deeper relationships or the ability to reveal a more significant unity. Coleridge turns an observation into verse to illustrate the unpoetic level of perception:

> Behold yon row of pines, that shorn and bow'd
> Bend from the sea-blast, seen at twilight eve.

These lines may have a little of the decorative characteristics of poetic speech in their rhythm and arrangement, but Coleridge can ascribe them equally suitably to 'a book of topography, or . . . a descriptive tour'. It seems, therefore, that incidentally standards for such literary works are being laid down, at the same time as they are clearly distinguished from the higher kind of creative writing, the poetic. Descriptive prose should faithfully copy and accurately record the images of nature; its use of words should be disciplined by such aims. The relevance of this view to Coleridge's—and other Romantic—topographical notes and journals recording tours and observations will be shown in

6

the following sections, but here I want to stress that he is not denigrating the virtues of faithful recording, nor dismissing out of hand the ability to achieve accuracy of observation. His aim is to distinguish these powers from the poetic gift. To bring home the difference, he roughly translates his two lines of observed appearance into a 'semblance of poetry':

> Yon row of bleak and visionary pines,
> By twilight glimpse discerned, mark! how they flee
> From the fierce sea-blast, all their tresses wild
> Streaming before them.

Clearly, what effects the change of status in Coleridge's opinion is the transference of 'human life' from the writer to the objects which he has seen. An evening spectacle of trees exposed to a strong wind has gained an emotional dimension, the reaction to the view having become a part of the thing seen. Just so, Coleridge goes on to argue, does Shakespeare succeed to an extraordinary degree in giving 'a dignity and a passion to the objects which he presents', so that 'they burst upon us at once in life and in power'. In no sense does his poetry distort or falsify the object. We are brought to a stronger realization of its essential nature because of the fusion with the emotional life of the mind contemplating it; and beside this impassioned perception involving the union of subject and object, the careful eye of the topographical observer seems less acute, because the object remains an object, and to that extent 'fixed and dead'.

Yet Coleridge's argument is undoubtedly elevating the subjective experience of the mind above the perception of the object. The emotionally reverberant units wrought by Shakespeare form the centre of his admiration for the dramatist as supreme exponent of imaginative power. The colouring of all circumstance, objects and external situations with the predominant passions of Othello or the agonies of Lear is extolled by Coleridge as the peak of creative achievement. His praise for Wordsworth in Chapter IV of the *Biographia* likewise emphasizes the modifying power of imagination in relation to observation, and the unifying light which the poet's mind sheds over all its materials. When offered to us by way of the animating medium of poetic vision, certainly the world is renewed, more vividly known—yet more striking is the whole quality of the creative mind's experience, for which that world is but the symbol and the means of utterance.

The crucial 'humanizing' function of art as he sees it is contained in the grounds Coleridge gives in Chapter XV for Shakespeare's supreme stature. In his notes 'On Poesy or Art' (1818), he makes his argument more explicit and universal. He claims here that art is 'the power of humanizing nature, of infusing the thoughts and passions of man into every thing which is the object of his contemplation; colour, form, motion, and sound, are the elements which it combines, and it stamps them into unity in the mould of a moral idea'.[5] The 'moral idea', the subjective vision or human consequence of creative contemplation, is the central feature to which the contributing images of nature are but the 'elements' it transfigures and the mode of its expression. They are broken down in order to be remade and reunified as icons rather than as the material objects commonly observed. Here another branch of Coleridge's theories becomes relevant—his frequent insistence that the artistic imitation of life is not to be equated with the ability to copy and reproduce phenomena exactly. Such copying lacks precisely that animating subjective perception, the union of mind with object, which he holds to be the purpose and point of art, and which leads us to the inner vision, not the external appearance. The artist's consciousness takes him away from the latter, transforming the merely seen into the fully realized. He must 'for a time abandon the external real in order to return to it with a complete sympathy with its internal and actual'.[6] The circuit from mind to object is completed by the object's becoming part of the subjective experience, part of the mind's knowledge of itself, where indeed the objective ceases to have a separate identity, all being 'internal and actual'. Nature has become thought and thought nature.

Coleridge, then, though not devaluing the world of sense phenomena, is consigning it to a subsidiary role in the all-important quest for the expansion of human self-consciousness and the divination of an inner moral cohesion in the universe. Until a thing is a symbol, it is to Coleridge less than itself; until it takes its place for him as a word in God's 'language of nature', it is deficient. His comments on the joys of chemistry in *The Friend* illustrate his approach as clearly as his praise for Shakespeare and Wordsworth. Given the phenomena of 'water and flame, the diamond, the charcoal, and the mantling champagne, with its ebullient sparkles', the mind of the chemist does not behold them as isolated and distinct. They are at once 'convoked and fraternized' by his theorizing. The excitement felt by most men (and he certainly speaks from personal enthusiasm) at the science of chemistry is rooted, Coleridge maintains, in its fundamental characteristic of revealing organization and unity. It appeals to the mind's deepest instinct for drawing the many into the One. Chemistry offers us 'the sense of a principle of connection given by the mind, and sanctioned by the correspondency of nature'. And he continues:

Hence the strong hold which in all ages chemistry has had on the imagination. If in Shakespeare we find nature idealized into poetry, through the creative power of a profound yet observant meditation, so through the meditative observation of a Davy . . . we find poetry, as it were, substantiated and realized in nature; yea, nature itself disclosed to us . . . as at once the poet and the poem![7]

Neither scientist nor artist therefore regards the world he encounters simply as a rag-bag of facts. What both pursue is the 'secret amity'[8] of all phenomena, the organic whole of the universe, and their energy of mind converts the world of material form into a spiritualized revelation of indwelling law and harmony of being. Genius in both spheres acts upon the feeling 'that body is but a striving to become mind'.[9] Such is the humanizing power of all imagination, exalting the subjectively perceived quality of relations over the mere recognition of miscellaneous objects belonging to a distinctly separate 'external real'. And as we saw earlier, centrally, in the field of the arts, these relations involve the emotional experience of man, humanizing phenomena in the sense of revealing the unity of subject and object in terms of our character as 'enjoying and suffering beings', to use Wordsworth's phrase.

To Coleridge, no imaginative utterance can be literally descriptive. The pine trees to the poet do not bend before the strong wind—they flee from it in fear. M. H. Abrams remarks in

9

The Mirror and the Lamp that most of the examples of poetic imagination which are cited in the *Biographia* discussion, 'fall under the traditional headings of simile, metaphor, and (in the supreme instances) personification'.[10] The instances Coleridge gives—and this is particularly striking in Chapter XV—are those showing 'the poet's power to animate and humanize nature by fusing his own life and passion with . . . objects of sense'. Like Wordsworth he abhorred the eighteenth-century convention which employed such devices merely as 'rhetorical convention', and so debased them. But in his philosophy of poetry, deeply committed to the reconciling of subject and object, they 'occupy a crucial position'. Personification for Coleridge, indeed, bears a peculiarly intense implication, suggesting the whole 'personalizing' process of creative activity, the assimilation of the external to the inner experience.

In his theory, therefore, Coleridge accepts the world of sense; but how important the act of observation is to him, how far he values the initial encounter with the 'external real', the object as such, the theory does not in detail show. He intimates that seeing pine trees in a wind can be an experience on two levels, those of prose and poetry, and for the purposes of his critical thought, the latter receives the stress as being the more penetrative kind of seeing. Yet he implies that the faithful record of impressions of nature, the descriptive note, is a preliminary to intense perception. If we do not see the blowing pine accurately, we shall not see more than this. He points out that genius, be it Shakespeare, Wordsworth or Davy, does keenly observe the world around and adds the powers of meditation and modifying imagination to that observation.

But we oversimplify if we draw conclusions only from this area of his work, for though we can recognize from the theory that he sees the external world as real but dependent, subordinate yet functionally important, we cannot learn from it how much this view is allied with love for that world and all its variety. To discover this we must turn to his descriptive writing.

DESCRIPTIVE PROSE

(i) 'Descriptive Tours and Books of Topography'

Coleridge's reference to topographical writing in Chapter XV reminds us that he was an avid reader of such books, and also that both he and the Wordsworths contributed readily to the genre. The instinct to record impressions of things seen—whether at home or on journeys—was one they shared with their age. Stimulated by the vogue of the 'picturesque', the Romantic version of descriptive writing was nevertheless distinctive and in some ways a reaction against formal and conventional appreciation of landscape features. Coleridge's individual handling of scenes and all visual phenomena can best be understood in relation to the achievements in the same field of William and Dorothy Wordsworth—the friends who shared his vision so closely at the period of their own most intense response to the world around them.

In these years, Dorothy Wordsworth kept her Alfoxden and Grasmere journals and wrote her more extended account of the 1803 tour in Scotland; she also recorded an 'Excursion on the Banks of Ullswater' in November 1805. All this is private writing, for the immediate circle, but Wordsworth himself developed their topographical prose by publishing in 1810, *A Guide through the District of the Lakes*, thereby eventually achieving a success which his poems could not rival.[11] I shall consider this work first, as it highlights some characteristically Romantic ways of seeing and conveying what was seen.

Although, as W. M. Merchant says in his introduction to the *Guide*,[12] there are signs of the picturesque vocabulary surviving in Wordsworth's prose, what is striking about his Lakeland tour is its insistence on seeing the district as it actually appears. Recognizable, that is, to an inhabitant, not merely to the visitor hastening from one 'station' to the next with appropriate ecstasies at each unfolding prospect. Wordsworth hopes to encourage 'more exact and considerate observation than . . . have hitherto been applied to local scenery',[13] and at the same time aims his guide, he says, at 'the *Minds* of Persons of taste, and feeling for Landscape'.[14] The conjunction here of an accurately observing eye with an appeal to mind and feeling helps to point the contrast between the aesthetic arrangements of scene so favoured by the picturesque travellers, designed to promote a response within a stock range of reactions, and the Romantic directness of eye, leading to a sensitive appreciation of the individual scene, unclassified and conforming to no preconceived rules of taste. At root, Wordsworth's approach is a practical exercise in seeing, any kind of emotional consequence being the reward for a genuine encounter with the reality of the landscape, from its geological to its human attributes. The layout of his *Guide* illustrates what might be termed the plain-sighted as opposed to the Lorraine-glass technique of observation. He begins with a 'view of the country as formed by nature', listing the features—'mountains, lakes, tarns, islands' and so on, then moves on to 'aspects of the country, as affected by its inhabitants'. His opening bird's-eye survey from Scafell conveys the skeleton form of the region—its valleys radiating from the centre 'like spokes from the nave of a wheel'[15]—and then he gradually fills in and animates the view with all its component parts, right down to the cottage chimneys. There are touches of a geological realism which would disconcert the rhapsodizing tourist. For example, he remarks that the constant flow of deposits from the mountains into the lakes will in time make the latter dwindle 'into numerous and insignificant pools; which, in their turn, will finally be filled up'.[16]

Only when the true nature and authentic appearance of the hills and valleys have been fully established does Wordsworth turn the discussion into one which directs judgment and seeks to preserve values. The third section is called 'Change, and rules of taste for preventing their bad effects'. Here too, he is realistic in accepting that the region must experience change, for economic and social reasons as well as from the erosions of weather and time. New plantations, new houses have to be accommodated, and he imposes rules of taste in accordance with these human enterprises, not as a regimentation of what views are to be seen and how. His aim is to preserve as far as possible the innate character of the area as he has shown it to be. The sense of place takes precedence throughout.

In *Tintern Abbey*, Wordsworth acknowledges that there was

a period of his life when visual pleasure in nature, a delight in 'colours and forms', was all in all to him. Although this time is long past by 1810, the survival of his ability to see keenly is proved by passages in the *Guide* which avowedly deal in 'exact observation', concerned to capture the visual quality of the district. For example, he describes the winter scene:

The oak-coppices, upon the sides of the mountains, retain russet leaves; the birch stands conspicuous with its silver stem and puce-coloured twigs; the hollies, with green leaves and scarlet berries, have come forth to view from among the deciduous trees . . . In place of the deep summer-green of the herbage and fern, many rich colours play into each other over the surface of the mountains; turf (the tints of which are interchangeably tawny-green, olive, and brown), beds of withered fern, and grey rocks, being harmoniously blended together.[17]

There is no interest here 'unborrowed from the eye'. Yet despite the *Guide*'s capacity to look at a patch of earth and report on it, this is a minor aspect of its attempt to communicate the sense of place. Wordsworth's intention to speak to the 'Mind' of persons with a feeling for landscape is responsible for the most typical prose in the work, which blends the visual with the emotional impact. He frequently draws attention to the relationship of the two, and the sequence from the thing seen to the subjective effect. Remarking on the special beauty of the lakes as they are seen on calm autumn days, he clinches the observation by emphasizing its power: by the 'aid' of the tranquil lakes, 'the imagination . . . is carried into recesses of feeling otherwise impenetrable'.[18] And in discussing climate, he makes the angle of approach clear—'climate, as influencing the feelings through its effect on the objects of sense'.[19] A particularly fine example of the *Guide*'s ability to bring together a due 'care for scientific analysis and description' and the 'claims of intuition',[20] occurs in the passage on 'those bodies of still water called Tarns'.[21] He first looks at them practically, and suggests how they came into being:

In the economy of Nature these are useful, as auxiliars to Lakes; for if the whole quantity of water which falls upon the mountains in time of storm were poured down upon the plains without intervention . . .

of such receptacles, the habitable grounds would be much more subject than they are to inundation.

Turning to the character of the tarns in the hills, he quickly introduces a human relationship into the descriptions. A mountain tarn is 'an acceptable sight to the mountain wanderer': first of all for scenic reasons—it brings variety to the view, and acts as a focal point for the eye. But as the visual impressions grow more detailed, so he draws on more atmospheric and emotional suggestion to convey the full character of these remote pools:

Some few have a varied outline, with bold heath-clad promontories; and, as they mostly lie at the foot of a steep precipice, the water, where the sun is not shining upon it, appears black and sullen; and, round the margin, huge stones and masses of rock are scattered; some defying conjecture as to the means by which they came thither; and others obviously fallen from on high—the contribution of ages! A not unpleasing sadness is induced by this perplexity, and these images of decay.

The bleakness of the treeless setting 'deepens the melancholy', and the whole scene modulates into an experience of Wordsworth's 'visionary dreariness' in the final section:

Nor is the feeling of solitude often more forcibly or more solemnly impressed than by the side of one of these mountain pools: though desolate and forbidding, it seems a distinct place to repair to; yet where the visitants must be rare, and there can be no disturbance. Water-fowl flock hither; and the lonely Angler may here be seen; but the imagination, not content with this scanty allowance of society, is tempted to attribute a voluntary power to every change which takes place in such a spot, whether it be the breeze that wanders over the surface of the water, or the splendid lights of evening resting upon it in the midst of awful precipices.

Without abandoning the geography of tarns, Wordsworth converts their physical appearance into a state of mind, transposing the scene into a subjective experience as his way of reaching a full recognition of its nature. His prose description, in short, is here moving rapidly towards his poetic vision.

The *Guide* shows that even where, as Coleridge suggests, we might expect to find the straightforward record of things seen,

the Romantic constantly feels the pressure of subjective interpretation, carrying him beyond the surfaces of colour and form
to the inner world. Intuitions of 'one life within us and abroad'
lead him to esteem the relation of observer to observed above
the dispassionate act of observing. Learning to look accurately
at nature is to Wordsworth only the preliminary to learning how
to feel.

But the looking is important. The *Guide* sees the Lakes with a
faithful eye and Wordsworth cares that it should do so. In his
sister's prose, the early nineteenth-century ability to see vividly
and to value this gift is demonstrated beyond doubt. Since her
writing is informal and for the most part spontaneous, it takes
us a step nearer Coleridge's Notebooks, as too does the knowledge that he saw with her eyes as intimately as he felt with
William.

Dorothy's sense of detail is acute and much of the life of her
descriptive writing flows from this. When she is confronted with
a set-piece of scenery, as for instance in the more spectacular
parts of the Highland tour in 1803, it is noticeable that she
falters in her attempt to convey what they saw, depending on the
stock vocabulary of 'a romantic effect', 'a sudden burst of
prospect', 'a beautiful image'. Or she gives up the struggle to
depict 'one of the most delightful prospects' with the verdict:
'my description must needs be languid; for the sight itself was
too fair to be remembered'.[22] But when she is dealing with a less
overwhelming landscape, especially one familiar to her, and
finds her eye able to seize on individual features, then her prose
achieves its characteristic purity of perception. Almost any of
the Grasmere journal entries illustrate it, and in the cumulative
effect of the day to day notes we discover that not merely detail,
but changing detail is the key to her seeing. The hourly
variations in the appearance of Grasmere and Rydal water; the
effects of weather and season on the hills or trees; shifting skies
and winds; flying birds or human passers-by: all such are the
ingredients of her records and transiency is the stimulus to her
precision. Thus Rydal on one August evening shows 'a curious
yellow reflection . . . as of cornfields', and the next day is 'a dark
mirror';[23] or it gleams 'with spear-shaped streaks of polished
steel'.[24] Grasmere is 'dappled with soft grey ripples',[25] it is a

'bright slate colour',[26] or the moon shines 'like herrings in the water'.[27]

Responding so keenly to the qualities which render a scene continually new, Dorothy is also arrested by the individuality of what she sees, rejoicing in the self-statement of all nature, from ranges of hills to particular trees or flowers. She incorporates a comment on such autonomy as a means of emphasizing the impact of the actual sight, its satisfying communication of its nature to her. 'Helm Crag rose very bold and craggy, a Being by itself';[28] and she sees the Coniston Fells 'in their own shape and colour'—hills 'all for themselves, the sky and the clouds, and a few wild creatures'.[29] With Mary and William on 24 November 1801, she was delighted at the sight of their 'favourite birch tree'. They stopped to gaze at it:

It was yielding to the gusty wind with all its tender twigs, the sun shone upon it, and it glanced in the wind like a flying sunshiny shower. It was a tree in shape, with stem and branches, but it was like a Spirit of water . . . The other birch trees that were near it looked bright and chearful, but it was a creature by its own self among them.[30]

'It was like a Spirit of water': this comparison in the midst of an intense concentration on the object indicates Dorothy's imaginative response, the modifying power active in her prose as well as the acute observation. Despite her sense of detail and of 'a Being by itself', the full life of her descriptions springs also from this further capacity, to perceive relationships between discrete items of nature and hence to convey a unity of scene, or to fix the immediate sight more sharply by a sudden vivid touch of simile. The latter is well shown in her account of a gay evening in a Highland cottage, when 'we caroused our cups of coffee', while

the smoke came in gusts, and spread along the walls and above our heads in the chimney, where the hens were roosting like light clouds in the sky; we laughed and laughed again . . . yet had a quieter pleasure in observing the beauty of the beams and rafters gleaming between the clouds of smoke. They had been crusted over and varnished by many winters, till, where the firelight fell upon them, they were as glossy as black rocks on a sunny day cased in ice.[31]

Drawing on the two nature images, she enhances the portrayal of the interior scene and spices it too with the suggestion of contrast, extending as well as concentrating our visual impressions. The simple level of observations recorded is surpassed. Even more does this apply to a description such as the following, belonging to the Alfoxden days, but typical of many throughout the journals:

The shapes of the mist, slowly moving along, exquisitely beautiful; passing over the sheep they almost seemed to have more of life than those quiet creatures. The unseen birds singing in the mist.[32]

Here mist, sheep and birds are no longer separate details noted down. They are all parts of an atmospheric unit, sheep and mist expressing each other's characteristics, and the birds, not merely voices in the scene, but becoming voices of it, articulating its quality. Dorothy, that is to say, like her brother, moves from the observed facts inwards to their implications or suggestions for the beholder. She creates a single vision out of the components of the scene, reaching a harmony of impression, and often, an emotional unity too. Again therefore the observed is invested with certain kinds of value by the subjective responses of the observer. A description is also a mood:

It is a breathless, grey day, that leaves the golden woods of autumn quiet in their own tranquillity, stately and beautiful in their decaying; the lake is a perfect mirror.[33]

'Tranquillity' is the pivot from external to internal, and the means of blending the two. Elsewhere her use of the term 'visionary' is the key to a psychological unifying which translates the spectacle of 'lake, clouds, and mists . . . all in motion to the sound of sweeping winds'[34] into a heightened experience, a special state of mind.

That Dorothy is well aware of the crucial meeting between the mind and 'striking' or 'simple' objects is established by her frequent references to the kindling of response, most of all in her more expansive accounts of the Highland journey. Soon after they set out in August 1803, she remarks that what she saw from the inn at Dumbarton 'was enough to set the mind at work':

17

It was no more than a smoky vessel lying at anchor, with its bare masts, a clay hut and the shelving bank of the river, with a green pasture above. Perhaps you will think that there is not much in this, as I describe it: it is true; but the effect produced by these simple objects, as they happened to be combined, together with the gloom of the evening, was exceedingly wild.[35]

And later, in another twilight scene, where 'all was solitary and huge', the blending of sky, water and mountains, together with the sudden appearance of a small boy wrapped in a plaid and shouting in Gaelic, 'was in the highest degree moving to the imagination'.[36] At other times, too, figures in a landscape form a stimulating picture, 'exciting thoughts and images' which make the scene representative rather than literal.

To both Wordsworths, then, visual experience was important. Seeing the world as it really was played a major part in their lives and in their writing, with Dorothy's the more acutely sensitive eye in catching the particular detail of the hour. But in their prose, we can recognize the incipient poetic transformation from external actuality to inner significance. So descriptive and topographical writing shows itself in practice to be, not sharply distinguished from poetry by its plainness of objective record, as Coleridge's theory implies, but already transitional from that first stage of observation towards what he saw as full imaginative status. This writing values the physical world of rocks, trees, animals and weather, and it reveals the Romantic effort to replace an affected, conditioned vision with a new directness of sensuous contact. But the 'inward eye' and its humanizing interpretations—atmospheric, emotional, moral— take precedence.

(ii) *The Notebooks*

'O Christ, it maddens me that I am not a painter or that Painters are not I!' (1.1495).[37] Thus Coleridge expresses his frustration at being unable to convey in words what he sees on the Scottish tour with the Wordsworths in September 1803. The exclamation is revealing in various ways: it suggests the intensity of his study of landscape and its features, his strong desire to preserve and communicate what he looks at so thoroughly, and it hints that he has ideas on the function of painting and does not find them adequately met.

He values particularly the directness of the painter's medium. On the same tour, he notes: 'The Head of Glen Nevish how simple for a Painter/ & in how many words and how laboriously, in what dim similitudes & slow & dragging Circumlocutions must I give it' (1.1489). Both media therefore are ways of describing what is before the eyes, a common purpose making them two aspects of one effort: 'Without Drawing I feel myself but half invested with Language' (1.1554). If it seems from these quotations that he regards the painter as superior to the verbal artist, the Notebooks as a whole suggest that the advantages of paint are confined to depicting the visual world and do not indicate a general creative superiority. His notes on some pictures by Sir George Beaumont, while showing him aware of technical values such as composition, line and colour, reveal also that his sense of the art-form is really secondary to the power it has to lead him back to the living scene. As Dr Coburn says, 'one notes his kinetic responses—a desire to cross bridges, pass under arches . . . and his sentimental and narrative inferences' (2.1899n). He will praise the 'noble Balance' of a picture, or the placing and colouring of a figure 'which lights up the whole Picture' (2.1899), but when Beaumont portrays a scene with a waterfall, for instance, Coleridge responds to it in a way almost indistinguishable from a personal encounter with a cataract:

A Waterfall, nay, a waterfury, a smoking Furnace of Fire!—four Trees forming three Forks on its right more than perpendicular jagged Bank,—with dripping Roots and lanky wet moss on the two highest Jags . . . a bush like Tree (not bushy) on the other Bank must needs have one of its branches in endless motion; for it is over the summit of the furious Fall. (2.1899,20)

A successful landscape picture to Coleridge, it would seem, is one which can stimulate him to convert the scene back into the original—by way of words. Despite his impatience with the oblique approach of verbal description and his irritation with the 'miserable scribble' of his own crude sketches, he is never reluctant to treat a picture as a point of departure for a verbal impression in which he can evoke and stress the animation of nature, only present in the picture by implication. And he says explicitly that it is the function of a painter to enhance response to the actual world: 'Paintings and Engravings send us back with new Eyes to Nature' (2.1907). Nature is central, and an artist who cannot provide the 'new Eyes'—because he lacks them himself—is inferior for that reason. Just to possess 'an eye' will lead only to the dead representations he labels 'copies' in his theory; the true visual artist is one who sees with an independent personal perception and so rouses his audience to do likewise. It is somewhat surprising that such a painter as Sir George Beaumont—an ardent supporter of the 'brown tree'—should prove capable of stimulating Coleridge's seeing. That he did so is evident from many admiring references to his work in the Notebooks.[38] But Coleridge also found authentic imaginative quality in the sonnets of Bowles, and this seems to be a parallel instance of his finding in the artist what he himself eagerly put there.

His reason for making detailed notes on the Beaumont pictures is an additional sign that Coleridge regarded such paintings as a means to a further artistic—as well as natural—end. There was a plan, first mentioned in a letter of September 1803 and followed up as far as the Notebook entries in February 1804, that he should produce some 'Translations from the Drawings' in the form of 'a moral Descriptive-poem', 'an Inscription', or 'a Tale' (2.1899n). The relationship suggested is analogous to Wordsworth's poetic use of Dorothy's prose and confirms the point that vivid seeing and the record of it is to these Romantics a preliminary to full imaginative activity, involving the 'humanization' of the sensuous world.

That 'moral Descriptive-poems' were to his taste, the Notebooks bear witness in the abundance of material they contain which was intended to find a home in such works. But before I consider this aspect of his prose, the fundamental implications of his references to painting can be related to other kinds of entry which feature prominently. Despite the 'labour' and the need for 'dragging Circumlocutions', Coleridge never gives up the attempt to capture what he sees verbally. He extols the painter's method simply because it meets his own evaluation of the importance of visual experience, epitomizing the immediacy of an encounter with the world outside self. Words may have their limitations as a means of expressing the thing seen, but his awareness that this is so is merely a measure of the premium he places on sensuous experience in itself, and he is always prepared to accept the challenge of painting in words. The urge to describe is as instinctive and powerful as the readiness to see. In Malta he is greatly pleased by some of the scenery and he at once resolves, 'I mean to go with my Pocket-book, & minute its features' (2.2449).

The pocket-book is always to hand as his verbal sketch-book; the descriptions find their place in those crammed receptacles for material awaiting further thought and development. The analogy between a painter's preliminary work and Coleridge's use of the notebook is brought out in Chapter X of the *Biographia Literaria*. Here he recalls his intentions during the Somerset days of writing a long poem to be entitled *The Brook*, and tells how he would walk 'on the top of Quantock' in preparation: 'with my pencil and memorandum book in my hand, I was *making studies*, as the artists call them . . . with the objects and imagery immediately before my senses'.[39] The 'studies' are not regarded as finished pieces of writing, but they are of obvious importance to him as sensuous records. To 'minute the features' is a necessary stage in Coleridge's total experience and assimilation of the world. His phrases, 'making studies' and 'minuting the features', indicate the kind of analytic passion which he brings to the task, giving a clue to the way in which his descriptive writing differs from Dorothy Wordsworth's.

Humphrey House says, 'the more one reads Coleridge's descriptions . . . the less easy it is to be convinced that he ever needed Dorothy Wordsworth as his tutor in seeing'.[40] Certainly Coleridge appreciated Dorothy's keen eye, 'watchful in minutest observation of nature'.[41] But a study of the Notebooks suggests that his appreciation is that of an equally perceptive fellow observer, one who shares her powers yet exerts them rather differently. On occasion, a Notebook entry is very close to Dorothy's journal:

Little wool-packs of white bright vapour . . . the Birds are singing in the tender Rain . . . The pillar of Smoke from the Chimney rises up in the Mist, & is just distinguishable from it. (1.1603)

It could well be that she influenced the delicacy of his seeing, but there is often a more vigorous engagement with his subject in Coleridge's records, a greater urgency in his encounter with natural phenomena. Comparing his account of the Scottish tour with Dorothy's, Dr Coburn sums up a difference which extends beyond the one year's example: 'Coleridge . . . loses himself . . . in the shapes and colours and movement of the landscape, trying with more energetic precision to articulate them' (1.1462n). He scrutinizes whatever presents itself to his eye with a determination to reach its full and exact nature, as if he feels a challenge to do so. It is noticeable how often he is driven to set down the characteristics of a changing scene— which indeed Dorothy does also. But where for her the changes are usually those from morning to evening, day to day, or seasonal variations, Coleridge strains more to catch the momentary shading of light, colour or form. He regards the continual dissolving of land- or seascape into new versions of itself as something which at once baffles and excites the eye. Looking at Ullswater in November 1799, he writes:

how shall I express the Banks waters all fused Silver, that House too its slates rainwet silver in the sun, & its shadows running down in the water like a column—the Woods on the right shadowy with Sunshine, and in front of me the sloping hollow of sun patched Fields . . . The Sun, it being just past noon, hangs over the Lake— clouded so that any but a weak eye might gaze on it—the clouds being in part bright white, part dusky Rain-clouds, with islets of blue Sky—How the scene changes—What tongues of Light shoot out from the Banks! (1.549)

The immediacy of the entries frequently derives from the strong intimations they give of transient, or even more, fleeting spectacle. He writes a commentary rather than a description:

Now the Hills are all in mist but the Vale all bathed & clean, one column of watry Sunshine falls upon the Grange . . . A pelting shower.—Clear;—& a road of silver brightness, from the woods far over the Lake to the other side of the Island.—Vanishes—beautiful appearance of moving mist over Newlands—in long dividuous flakes the interspaces filled up by a thinner mist—all in sunlight . . . (1.808)

His alertness to subtleties and complexities of colour in nature

22

was stimulated by the Lake country, as Dr Coburn notes (1.783n), and his records of skyscapes in the region touch Turner's perception of colour qualities, relationships, and effects as the two following examples will illustrate. In August 1800, he observes the sky at sunset:

> river of amber mist athwart the green . . . a rich satteny yellow on the green ridge . . . one *small* break of a dusky marone . . . broken masses, red & fluky . . . —over head marbled Sky with under clouds of pink . . . (1.783)

And in the same month, a more extensive evening scene with a time progression and change of light:

Walla Crag purple red, the lake a deep dingy purple blue . . . As we turned round on our return, we see a moving pillar of clouds, flame & smoke, rising, bending, arching, and in swift motion . . . I scarcely ever saw in the sky such variety of shapes, & colors, & colors floating over colors.—Solemnly now lie the black masses on the blue firmament of—not quite night—for still at the foot of Bassenthwaite there is a smoky russet Light.—Tis 9 oclock. (1.781)

The energy of Coleridge's visual activity can be gauged from such descriptions of scenes which he strove to render as completely as possible before they were gone for ever. But his thoroughness, the resolution to let nothing escape his scrutiny, is apparent in the abundance of detail which the Notebooks record, whether of evanescent effects, more permanent features of nature, or some combination of the two. Dr Coburn remarks on the 'many attempts in the notebooks to describe clouds' (1.315n) and 'the struggle to describe water' which goes on as an aspect of the 'many detailed attempts to describe colour' (2.2067n). All these are elusive, ever-present yet always changing features, and he is specially attracted to such phenomena. The whole tendency of his mind is to achieve a more precise, a more particularized 'minuting' of everything he sees. His habit when faced with a scene, his editor says, is to 'take his bearings' in a 'sweeping' view, then to observe closely 'the detail at his feet' (2.2171n). The method reflects one of his philosophic statements in the Notebooks, where he admits the fascination of the particular—'the very thing'—over the general:

23

at first we are . . . delighted with *generalities* of Nature which can all be expressed in dignified words/ but afterwards becoming more intimately acquainted with Nature in her detail we are delighted with *distinct* vivid ideas, and with vivid ideas most when made distinct/ & can most often forgive & sometimes be delighted with even a low image from art or low life when it gives you the very thing by an illustration . . . (2.2484)

Clearly to Coleridge the art of depicting 'Nature in her detail' in words is inseparable from the loving recognition of that detail. The 'dignified' word may well be the vague one, and his Notebooks duly repudiate any stock vocabulary of description, yielding numerous examples of distinct perception captured in vivid expression, either directly or by use of a 'low image'. To fix the individual character of anything, from a thistle to a spider, from urine to a wave of the sea, he exerts first his considerable powers of visual concentration, then his extensive verbal resources. The result is a series of descriptive notes which unite analysis with the sensuous experience of the object, living or inanimate. There are new trees and flowers seen for the first time in Sicily and Malta: the gazae or gaggia tree—'pendulous Branches, seed pods black at the same time with the orange yellow flower, a little daisy-like tuft of silky hair' (2.2195); the 'beautiful Milk Thistle'—with 'the milk-blue white veins or fibres up & athwart its dark green Leaves' (2.2519); and, meticulously studied, the stone-crop flower:

exactly a star . . . 6 petals equi-distant, most tender & delicate purple, with a white ground, as it were, attempting to gleam thro' it/ and the little round of the o in the centre of the flower are of darkest crimson, very far darker than the barberry-shaped leaves. (2.2564)

Even when the note becomes strictly analytic, to the point sometimes of breaking down the object into numbered parts, still the report is fresh with the 'distinct vivid idea', not a dead catalogue. 'The wave itself', noted on the Malta voyage, is exactly that: 'its crown of foam/ its larger Hollows—its puckers —its wrinkles, & 5th, its dimples & sunshine' (2.1995). Likewise a waterfall, seen in 1803:

An Apron, of tressy water/ 2. a steep Slope of leaping billowy water, 3. a grand Plunge, an arch of water, 4. a long Elbow of a narrow

Torrent, with many a plunging Waterbreak, 5 & last, a direct perpendicular Fall adown a smooth Rock, which no where project- ing is passively parallel with the stream . . . (1.1694)

The tireless search for the exact report of the 'very thing' rules the use of images in the descriptions, as we might expect from his recognition that 'low images' can have this function. But frequently his choice of image shows too the instinctive tendency of his mind to humanize nature: his eye or ear is firmly concentrated on the immediate object or creature commanding his attention, but the way to render its character precisely is, for Coleridge, to make the human connection. The yellow-hammer sings 'like one working on steel, or the file in a brazier's Shop' (1.1168); the singing redbreast 'opens and shuts the upper and lower mandible like a tiny pair of the finest scissors!' (2.2992). The moon undergoing eclipse 'was *all* like a round of silver completely lost in egg-tarnish', brightening again gradually 'as by laborious Scouring' (2.2610); and a night sky shows

black Clouds, two or three dim untwinkling Stars, like full stops on damp paper—& large Stains & Spreads of sullen White, like a tunic of white Wool seen here & there thro' a torn & tattered Cloak of Black . . . (1.1648)

Long wet bracken lies 'strait dangling, from the mossy stone- hillocks like an unkempt red brown Hair' (1.1160); while he enjoys himself with ribald elaboration at the sight of a road which strikes him as 'a sort of suture' in the 'round fat back side of a Hill' (1.555). Though here it might seem that the feminine resemblance rather supersedes the original observation in his interest, usually images of the kind quoted are intended to be merely methods of emphasizing and crystallizing the nature of the thing encountered. They are tools aiding the mapping of the world of sense and are subordinate to that world.

The object is not always so dominant in the Notebooks, and imagery with human bias gives the first hint of the way in which Coleridge likes to transmute the data from the physical world as he collects it. He is not content simply to see, however accurately and fully; for him, as for the Wordsworths, the sensuous record in itself is only a stimulus, a stage in a vision which goes beyond what eye and ear report, to discover a more suggestive importance and power. Nevertheless, before I try to show how this common tendency operates in Coleridge's mind and in his prose, I would stress again that sharp visual experience of the world is indispensable for this Romantic group. They welcomed the world of sense as a gift to be endlessly contemplated; and the energy of their seeing must not be passed over casually because we know it is a means to an end. Enough has been given from the Notebooks already, as well as from the Wordsworths' prose, to support the fundamental point that they savoured the variety, large and small, around them; in Coleridge's notes, however, the intensity of study is so marked that it deserves more illustration before I move beyond it. As Humphrey House claims, he shows 'a kind of organized and detailed watching with which he has not always been credited'.[42] A Notebook entry which demonstrates the readiness of his eye and its untiring alertness to close detail occurs during the Scottish tour. After a scrupulous time spent 'minuting the features' of a new mountain scene, he is satisfied, seeing 'there was not probably anything more to be noticed', and consciously relaxes his attention. Yet the observations which follow are scarcely those of an idle viewing:

> now my mind being as it were leisurely and of[f] the stretch with what delight did I look at a floatage of Shadows on the water, made by the wavelets of the Stream, with what delight that most exquisite net at the bottom/ sandy + pebbly river, all whose loops are wires of sunshine, gold finer than silk, beside yon Stone the Breeze seems to have blown them into a Heap, a rich mass of light, light spreading from the loop holes into the interstices ... (1.1489)

He adds a moral: 'O we turn from novelties & rarities to old Delights & simple Beauty!' Feelings of delight—whether in familiar or newly discovered sights—are for Coleridge inseparable from rigorous scrutiny. His joy in the object urges him to the closest possible itemizing of its characteristics, and the itemizing increases his joy. In his passion for 'the very thing', he is impatient of accidental associations. 'I have the faintest pleasure in things contingent & transitory', he says, deciding that he would not be able to do justice to Shakespeare's mulberry tree as a tree, because the distracting thought of its associations would prevent him 'as a whole man losing myself in the flexures of its Branches & interweaving of its Roots' (2.2026). Looking at birch trees 'of all shapes & Twisture', he declares that as a painter he would 'study' the birch—'it should be my only Tree' (1.1495).

While he has his favourite landscapes and trees and cherishes certain aspects of nature on which he bestows repeated study, Coleridge's appetite for sense experience is markedly catholic. He had of course particular reason during much of his life to regard the objective scene with more than ordinary attention, as Dr Coburn sympathetically perceives: 'the attempts to hold on to (by observing and noting) the real world in the very moments of being drugged against it are numerous and among the most poignant things in the notebooks' (1.1767n). But both the need for contact with external phenomena, and the sheer joy of 'observing and noting' to be found in him at all times are only general emotional incentives for an activity which can yield more specific insights into the workings of Coleridge's mind. He is open to all the impressions his senses bring, whatever their source, because he possesses in full measure the artist's zest for the variety of creation together with the scientist's curiosity about it. He writes as an analytic painter, and as a scientist of sensitive vision. The Notebooks exhibit this combination in their whole nature, and in the individual entries they frequently display the union of the two kinds of awareness. Many examples have been given in extracts I have quoted; it is impossible to avoid so fundamental a characteristic. But two passages may be added to consolidate the point. The first shows that, given the keen eye and the readiness to substitute an attentive instead of a prejudiced approach, nothing is unworthy:

What a beautiful Thing Urine is, in a Pot, brown yellow, transpicuous, the Image, diamond shaped of the Candle in it, especially, as it now appeared, I having emptied the Snuffers into it, the Snuff floating about, & painting all-shaped Shadows on the Bottom. (1.1766)

The artist sees colours and effects of light, the scientist details carefully the part played by each constituent in producing them, and the note blends the two kinds of observation. Similarly, recording a piece of spider-behaviour, he responds to the creature in its delicate buoyancy of movement and appearance:

On St Herbert's Island I saw a large Spider with most beautiful legs floating in the air on his Back by a single Thread which he was spinning out, and still as he spun, heaving in the air, as if the air beneath were a pavement elastic to his Strokes/—from the Top of a very high Tree he had spun his Line, at length reached the Bottom, tied his Thread round a piece of Grass, & re-ascended, to spin another/ a net to hang as a fisherman's Sea net hangs in the Sun & Wind, to dry. (1.1598)

Once we recognize the element of scientific curiosity in so many of the descriptive entries in the Notebooks, we begin to modify the idea that Coleridge might be just an accurate observer of the world, one brilliantly capturing the miscellany as it comes. Passionately interested though he is in all detail from stones to clouds, this is only one aspect of his interest, and not the centre of it. He would be unfaithful to his philosophic self were it otherwise, and false too to his concept of what constitutes a genuine scientific interest in phenomena. In a letter to Thomas Poole he repudiates the thought of the universe as a 'mass of *little things*',[43] while in the section of *The Friend* referred to earlier,[44] he sees the scientist as one alert to 'secret amity', the laws unifying all nature. Hence it is not surprising to find a strong current of intellectual speculation coursing through the Notebooks, giving many entries the status of experiments, not merely descriptions. There is the constant pressure of a questioning mind at work. His descriptive accuracy springs from delight in the object but it also serves the larger purpose, the desire to find that object's place, which in its turn indicates the search for a comprehensive understanding of an organic universe. Coleridge's universe is one of relationships, not things, and his Notebooks, for all their tributes to the thing-as-itself, confirm that bias.

The recurrent notes on candles, their flames and reflections bring out his admiration for their appearance—they are 'beautiful forms . . . so often gazed at' (2.2388). But the gaze is analytic, the appearance is patiently broken down and its components enumerated:

1. The beautiful amber edges of the flame, including the yellow-white flame. 2. The unsteadiness of the outer flame; but which is most often the *head* of an Halbert . . . (2.2934)

Such study of the shape and colouring of different parts of the flame is connected with his reading of Joseph Priestley's *Opticks* (1772). His innate readiness to think about visual phenomena and the action of light was encouraged to further theoretical and practical development by his acquaintance with technical works of this kind.[45] The 'inquiring spirit' explicitly motivates entries such as the following of November 1801:

The Two Candles on the Table—Reflections in the Looking Glass, over each cone of Light a compact Brush of Misty Light ejaculated— & a broader & somewhat less compact & somewhat differently coloured Beam of Light running over athwart high across the flames of the 2 cones—Transition—Dimness—why then, the Proportion being the same? (1.1024)

Observation and sensitive recording of the thing seen lead on to speculation. Questions arising out of what is seen are a commonplace in the Notebooks, the writer's mind stimulated by its own descriptions to ask how and why, seeking the laws of behaviour rather than resting with the isolated phenomenon. And the intellectual energy does far more than turn candle-flames into problems of physics, chemistry and optics. Coleridge's perception leaps further to the inner world of man, the emotional and moral life with its more enigmatic laws of behaviour. Here is the centre of his interest, in the Notebooks as everywhere.

Coleridge's descriptive prose, in short, shows the same tendency as the Wordsworths'. Although the intellectual pressure is uniquely his, the movement it promotes is still from the outer to the inner world, transfiguring fact into symbol. The candle entries illustrate this type of movement. Dr Coburn notes that his interest in the single or double flames of candles is linked with his awareness of solitude and his desire for a 'marriage of souls' (2.2934n). In 1795, he adds 'Picture of Hymen' to the following entry:

The flames of two Candles joined give a much stronger Light than both of them separate—evid. by a person holding the two Candles near his Face, first separate, & then joined in one. (1.13)

In 1796, the *Ode to the Departing Year* contains the lines,

> where, his two bright torches blending
> Love illumines Manhood's maze.
>
> (17–18)

The assimilation of fact into human context is complete. Frequently the Notebooks exhibit for us the transitional moment where Coleridge exercising his acute powers of observation becomes Coleridge thinking and feeling, arriving at insights which are destined for development in his poems and philosophic writings. Because they are jottings of such immediacy, the entries retain all the excitement of the process and demonstrate how the intensity of the sensuous experience generates the perceptions which supersede it. In the following description of a winter scene with a waterfall, the descriptive vocabulary itself yields a paradox which for Coleridge is philosophically significant:

The waterfall at the head of the vale . . . white, stedfast, silent from Distance/—the River belonging to it, smooth, full, silent—the Lake into which it empties also silent/ yet the noise of waters every where . . . and the pillar of smoke/ the smooth winter fields—the *indistinct* Shadows in the Lake are all eloquent of Silence . . . (1.1784)

Were he not so intent on the scene, and so stretched to record it accurately, the implications would not emerge. Dr Coburn remarks: 'Extremes meeting and opposites reconciled—not here a theory but something perceived through the senses' (1.1784n); the theory is present, but alive within the experience. Usually in the entries, however, it is not so implicit. Coleridge shows himself aware of the relationship between the world of sense and the mind, and the awareness forms part of his note and much of its point. He ponders on the intangibility of the boundary between sensation and emotion, looking at the night sky:

deep Sky is of all visual impressions the nearest akin to a Feeling/

it is more a Feeling than a Sight/ or rather it is the melting away and entire union of Feeling & Sight. (2.2453)

To see the sky properly is simultaneously to know it with the eye as 'the inside of a sapphire Bason' and with the mind as 'immensity' (2.2346). It is always the reinforcement of the initial sense impression with the enlarging concept, or the deepening feeling, which stimulates him to excitement, and 'minuting the features' works as a means to this end. There may be a sudden flash of simile, catching the moment of illumination which effects the extension from a 'nature note' to a perception: 'the beards of Thistle & dandelions flying above the lonely mountains like life' (1.799); or a specific memoranda for poetic use—'Leaves of Trees upturned by the stirring wind in twilight—an image for paleness from affright' (1.714); or, one stage removed from sense impressions, a more involved analogy applying cosmic physics to morality:

Motives from Religion like the light from the Sun—the earth principally heated from within itself—the Sun the cause of winter & summer by a very small quantity of heat in addition to that residing in the earth. (1.129)

Evidence of the degree to which his attention concentrated on a detail rouses his other faculties and provides him with enduring food for meditation, not just a moment's insight, is given in the two Notebook accounts of the eddying river Greta, first as he watched it from a bridge 'near its fall into the Tees', and then as he remembered it. His immediate description in October 1799 nets the visual qualities, and shows how they excite him until the first step from fact to symbol is taken:

Shootings of water threads down the slope of the huge green stone —The white Eddy-rose that blossom'd up against the stream in the scollop, by fits & starts, obstinate in resurrection—It *is the life* that we live. (1.495)

Four years later, he returns to the 'Eddy-rose' when he makes some entries in the Notebook under the heading 'Images'. He repeats the description and relives the experience, but expands the implications of the sight. Several kinds of speculation were generated by it, and its abiding vividness in his memory is inseparable from the thought it inspired:

The *white rose* of Eddy-foam, where the stream ran into a scooped or scolloped hollow of the Rock in its channel—this Shape, an exact white rose, was for ever overpowered by the Stream rushing down in upon it, and still obstinate in resurrection it spread up into the Scollop, by fits and starts, *blossoming* in a moment into [a] full Flower. —Hung over the Bridge, & musing considering how much of this Scene of endless variety in Identity was Nature's—how much the living organ's!—What would it be if I had the eyes of a fly!—what if the blunt eye of a Brobdignag! (1.1589)

The inter-relationship between the world and the observer which he glances at here is a study fundamental to Coleridge. It governs all his sensuous experience, so that there can never be for him a series of dissociated impressions, each one pleasingly complete. The physical facts stir him, because there is 'one life within us and abroad', one set of laws which nature exemplifies and to which we respond; or which we may create for ourselves and then discover mirrored in nature. Aware of the alternatives and eager to reconcile them, Coleridge continually demonstrates in his Notebooks that the deepest instinct of his mind is to unify nature. Even in prose notes, the distinct painting of facts— brilliantly indulged though it is—is only a preliminary to the relating of those facts to each other, and to their absorption into the moral and intellectual life. The Wordsworths react similarly, as William converts the mountain tarn into a state of mind, and Dorothy fuses mist, sheep and quietness into one atmospheric unit. Coleridge, typically, as well as putting fact into a symbolic role, penetrates straight to the laws governing mind and universe. Time and again, he seizes on what his senses offer him as evidence for such unifying principles. The harmony of opposites; 'endless variety in Identity'; the organic relation of the many to the One: these concepts repeatedly spring from his contemplation of natural features. For example, flocks of birds, waves in the sea, or a range of hills fascinate him in their display of a multitude, even an endlessly changing multitude, for ever suggesting a coherent unit. He watches a flight of linnets, noting their 'rise and fall . . . so that while one was rising, another was falling', and the intricacy of their motion, 'all at once in one beautiful Whole, like a Machine' (2.1851). Looking at the landscape near Messina in Sicily he exclaims:

I am more & more enamoured of the marvellous playfulness of the Surface of the Hills/ such swellings, *startings*, sinkings, and yet all so combined as to make it impossible to look at as many/ no! it was a manifold *One*! (2.2705)

And while taking full visual pleasure in the 'blue, yellow, green, & purple green Sea, with all its hollows & swells', he feels as he looks,

the mind within me . . . struggling to express the marvellous distinctness & unconfounded personality of each of the million millions of forms, & yet the undivided Unity in which they subsisted. (2.2344)

Coleridge's Notebooks certainly show that nature, in Humphrey House's phrase, has its own 'proper interest'[46] for him. His starting-point is the 'strength of impression' made on his senses by the external world, and this strength is considerable. But the moral, emotional and intellectual bonds which the struggling mind recognizes between itself and that world, and the ability it possesses to incorporate the objective phenomena into its own life—these are for him the salient consequences of observation. It is not surprising that he thought William Bartram's *Travels through North and South Carolina* (1791) 'a *delicious* book', and called its contents 'a series of poems', for Bartram also unites a sensitive eye with a moral vision. He describes in vivid detail trees, animals, landscapes, but lit by the humanizing light.[47] And if Bartram's prose is moving towards poetry, this is persistently the case in Coleridge's own Notebooks. They exemplify their author's absolute conviction that 'body' is constantly 'striving to become mind', and they reveal the energy which he devotes to bringing about the metamorphosis. A series of notes in January 1805 begins by observing the moon with a halo, moves on to meditations on 'magnitude', 'substance' and 'spaciousness', and finally arrives at thought on the soul (2.2402). Such is the progression throughout. The adventure of descriptive prose for Coleridge is precisely that the better it is executed, the more it will transcend itself and begin to yield the fruits of poetry. 'Gazing long & stedfastly' (1.1559), seeing acutely, is the first step in piercing the barriers between subject and object, so that the latter can become a language for the 'moral idea', the Creator's utterance. In nature humanized, we find a mirror; what we recognize as we read is our own significance. One last extract from the Notebooks will eloquently confirm this conclusion to which all the entries lead:

In looking at objects of Nature while I am thinking, as at yonder moon dim-glimmering thro' the dewy window-pane, I seem rather to be seeking, as it were *asking*, a symbolical language for something within me that already and forever exists, than observing anything new. Even when that latter is the case, yet still I have always an obscure feeling as if that new phenomenon were the dim Awaking of a forgotten or hidden Truth of my inner Nature/ It is still interesting as a Word, a Symbol! It is . . . the Creator! (2.2546)

POEMS

Coleridge complained of Erasmus Darwin's poetry that it strikes the reader as 'a succession of Landscapes or Paintings', which means that it 'arrests the attention too often, and so prevents the rapidity necessary to pathos'. He compared the poems to a painter's studies of beautiful objects (1.132). In other words, Darwin's work struck Coleridge as being notebook material, the preliminary to poetry rather than the finished product. The notebook is the proper place as he sees it for vivid observation as such, for the clearest visual account of the objects of nature. If attention remains fixed on the object described, the result, however brilliant, is not a poem but a 'study' which might lead to a poem. The eye's function poetically is to release the mind and stimulate feeling, not to halt response at its visual data.

Coleridge's own poems, seen in relation to the Notebooks, bear out his ideas on the differences between descriptive and creative writing. Like Wordsworth when his poetry is compared with the *Guide to the Lakes*, or with Dorothy's journals, Coleridge moves firmly away from report into a subjective universe, where sensuous detail is absorbed. His poetic world is the world of self, explored either directly or dramatically. The poems search into the hidden truth of his inner nature, and in them the reading of natural objects as a symbolic language is accepted as the norm. *Kubla Khan* may stand as an extreme example

[handwritten annotations: "describes", "Coleridges personal", "detail"]

of natural features subsumed by an esoteric personal vision, wrought into a tense but patterned relationship and through it reflecting the creating mind in turmoil and repose. Fountain, river, sunny dome and caves of ice are all properties rather than phenomena: they are disembodied, being so totally imbued with psychological implication. In *The Ancient Mariner* too, where detail is so important to the impact of the narrative, there is no mistaking the manner of its importance. Although scenes are vividly evoked, they reach us as aspects of the Mariner's experience; no poem telling the story of a voyage could be less of a detached descriptive account of travel. Events natural and supernatural, visions of sea and seraphs, blend together easily with no jolt to credibility, because they all express the mind of the Mariner in its anguished evolution. He is not encouraging the Wedding Guest to visualize geographically the regions in which he sailed, nor is he teaching him to distinguish an albatross from other sea birds; he is unfolding a tale of psychological nightmare and conversion, the history of what brought him to his present state.

These poems in their rather specialized ways show the subjective in control, making all things express inner nature. The abundance of interpretation they have attracted testifies to their possessing a symbolistic rather than a factual potency. Many of Coleridge's poems, however, concern themselves more explicitly with the relationship of mind and world. They exhibit the interplay between the two which leads to subjective supremacy and they declare the poet's awareness that such is the goal. Objects of nature present in the poems are seen undergoing the process of assimilation. Works both crude and sophisticated share these characteristics and if we look at some examples of each we shall see more clearly what happens to the world of sense when it leaves Coleridge's Notebooks and enters his poems. In the more naïvely constructed, his intention and the mechanics of bringing it about are usefully exposed to view, while in mature achievements such as *Frost at Midnight* the nature of his success and of the reader's pleasure yield the evidence.

Fears in Solitude (1798) and *Reflections on Having Left a Place of Retirement* (1795) both contain lines of careful observation which might have come straight from the Notebooks. He describes in

the former exactly how 'fresh and delicate' the green of the
valley is, comparing it with 'unripe flax',

> When, through its half-transparent stalks, at eve,
> The level sunshine glimmers with green light.

(8–11)

And recalling the 'place of retirement', he sees again

> The bare bleak mountain speckled thin with sheep;
> Grey clouds, that shadowing spot the sunny fields.

(30–1)

To the reader, these descriptive moments may well stand out as
islands of quality in the midst of verbally undisciplined seas of
feeling and 'reflections', for neither poem can be said to display
as a whole Coleridge's powers of control and judgment. But
undoubtedly he himself regards the passages of visual appeal as
stimuli rather than self-sufficient achievement. Both poems
evoke a sense of locality as a way of generating feeling and
meditation, relating the places being looked at or remembered
to the state of mind which is the real territory of the works.
Fears in Solitude begins with the 'green and silent spot, amid the
hills', but its physical character is quickly interpreted in terms
of its effect on the onlooker. "'Tis a quiet spirit-healing nook'
(12), conducive to reverie, so that the senses are abandoned for
a dream of 'better worlds' (26). Thus there is a rapid transition
from the thing seen to its emotional consequence; the 'singing
lark' is still heard, but as 'an angel in the clouds' (27–8). After
using the landscape to hint at felicities beyond itself, the poem
employs it more dramatically to develop an argument by contrast. The peace of the silent hills is threatened by invasion, 'the
thunder and the shout' (36), and equally, the corruption of the
nation violates such natural beauty. These themes are dwelt
upon at length and the local immediacy is dissolved in an
excited tirade of grief, indignation and exhortation. But it was
the scene which, by moving him, launched the poet into the
revelation of his forebodings and 'filial fears' (198) at the state
of England, and the poem finally returns to the 'soft and silent
spot' (208), once more effecting a change of mood by means of
it. Turning from the idea of political England, he addresses his
'Mother Isle' (176) again as a geographical presence, dear to

him as teacher and guide. After a general invocation to the 'divine and beauteous island' (193–4), he arrives back at the specific place which on this evening represents the deeply mellowing influence of natural beauty. Looking down from the brow of the hill at 'beloved Stowey' (221), he is restored to calm. The poem ends where it began, expressing gratitude to the 'green and silent dell' for making the heart receptive to love and concerned for 'human kind' (228–32).

Jerkily managed and poorly balanced though it is, *Fears in Solitude* displays a structure typical of Coleridge. So too does *Reflections on Having Left a Place of Retirement*. The evocation of the 'pretty Cot' (1) and its surroundings is inseparable from the poet's somewhat sentimental recollection of his serenity while living there. He contrasts that peace with the sterner present, when he feels it necessary to 'fight the bloodless fight Of Science, Freedom and the Truth in Christ' (61–2), an obligation for which the 'window-peeping Rose' and 'Myrtles fearless of the mild sea-air' (66–7) are unsuitable symbols. Again the poem begins and ends in contemplation of a specific place, the cottage representing a desirable state of mind as well as a way of life, to which he looks back in personal memory and forward in general social aspiration: 'Let Thy Kingdom come!' (71).

Furthermore, both poems affirm explicitly that nature is to be regarded as an expression of God. In this most fundamental sense, its features are symbols and are to be read as the infinite Mind's way of communicating with the finite and of developing moral responses. 'Nature itself is to a religious observer the art of God', Coleridge says in 'On Poesy or Art',[48] and in these poems he writes as a religious observer. The great bowl of landscape laid out below the 'stony Mount' (27) in the *Reflections* is conveyed as an immediate visual experience—'*Here* the bleak mount . . . the Channel *there*, the Islands and white sails' (29–36), but it fires his mind as a vision of 'Omnipresence': 'God, methought, Had built him there a Temple' (38–9). The moral consequence, not the spectacle itself, forms the climax to the passage:

> No *wish* profan'd my overwhelméd heart.
> Blest hour! It was a luxury,—to be!
>
> (41–2)

37

In *Fears in Solitude*, the beauty of the landscape leads the 'wise' man to a state of 'meditative joy', which in its turn enables him to find 'Religious meanings in the forms of Nature' (23–4). And the belief in a direct bridge leading from what the senses behold to spiritual insights is patriotically asserted in another passage of the poem, where he declares that from Britain's 'quiet dales . . . rocks and seas', he has drunk in all his intellectual life,

> All sweet sensations, all ennobling thoughts,
> All adoration of the God in nature,
> All lovely and all honourable things,
> Whatever makes this mortal spirit feel
> The joy and greatness of its future being.
>
> (185–91)

So the mind is developed by the body's encounter with physical phenomena, and as a complementary process, the phenomena are themselves spiritualized and given a more exalted subjective life.

A reciprocal movement, therefore, between outer world and inner is articulated in a rather bald way in the two poems so far considered. It is exploited with a far more assured artistry in *Frost at Midnight* and some other poems, but it is central to Coleridge's work as a poet whether or not it inspires him to impressive creation. *Fears in Solitude* sums up his attitude when he notes the effect of a 'burst of prospect' (215). Despite the picturesque phrase, he stresses that the impact is rewarding, not to the discerning eye, but to the eager mind with which the view converses,

> giving it
> A livelier impulse and a dance of thought!
>
> (219–20)

The orientation towards the intellectual life and the role of the outer world in feeding the inner is here unmistakably one which delights Coleridge.

His relation with other human beings is also poetically important in the movement from sense to emotional experience. Fully displayed in *This Lime-Tree Bower* and *The Nightingale*, his desire to increase his response to nature by incorporating the imagined reponse of others is more primitively shown in a poem of 1796: *To a Young Friend*, 'on his proposing to domesticate with the Author'. First describing the local scene as it unfolds to him during a solitary ascent of the 'green mountain' (2), Coleridge then repeats the account of its pleasures as if visiting them with a companion, insisting that all would be enriched by the enthusiastic presence of the young friend. Favourite spots would be doubly enjoyed if they were shared experiences. Observation would be sharpened, he suggests, and this is borne out when his first description of a rowan by a stream is compared with the second. The first is sketched in general colour and motion only:

> 'mid the summer torrent's gentle dash
> Dance brighten'd the red clusters of the ash.
>
> (6-7)

But the second is fixed with more of the Notebook alertness for the 'very thing':

> O then 'twere loveliest sympathy, to mark
> The berries of the half-uprooted ash
> Dripping and bright.
>
> (20-2)

'Loveliest sympathy' is the theme of the whole poem; notably, its power to stimulate moral, not merely visual reactions to the landscape.[49] Reiterating the idea of nature's direct influence on the moral life, he offers a near-maudlin vision of the perfect existence when two minds in concert drink their fill of truth:

> There, while the prospect through the gazing eye
> Pours all its healthful greenness on the soul,
> We'll smile at wealth, and learn to smile at fame,
> Our hopes, our knowledge, and our joys the same,
> As neighbouring fountains image each the whole.
>
> (67-72)

Coleridge reinforces his own response to 'healthful greenness' when he mirrors his experience in another person. He may well impose his vision quite arbitrarily on the young friend, or any friend, but poetically, the device enables him to assert with double stress and more resources for variety, that nature works upon the human mind and alchemizes it. Two or more minds in a poem reacting with similar gain to one view, or one bird singing, ensure that such subjective consequence is sufficiently valued. The emphasis clearly falls on it and there is no risk that the poem will isolate any descriptive 'study' for its own sake, as the Notebook alone might legitimately do. True poetic proportion, and connection leading to 'rapidity of pathos' are guaranteed. For the reader, the experience of sense impressions assimilated into a mental world by whose light they are to be interpreted is inescapable.

What matters is how the landscapes live in the minds which receive them. Their subjective enshrinement is their high destiny, as Coleridge shows in several ways in *This Lime-Tree Bower* (1797). He follows the method of *To a Young Friend*, suggesting a double encounter with the scene of the walk. His knowledge of the route is renewed as he imagines his friends discovering its attractions for the first time. But as he describes what they are seeing, he shows how completely the 'branchless ash', the 'long lank weeds' and the whole 'wide landscape' (40) belong to his inner vision: they are properties of his mental world, imbued with his personal atmosphere. The poem's descriptions in their detail keep the alertness of the Notebook, but they are touched with what Dorothy Wordsworth would call a 'visionary' quality. The 'roaring dell', for instance, is nearer to *Kubla Khan*'s 'deep romantic chasm' than to a rambler's report:

> The roaring dell, o'erwooded, narrow, deep,
> And only speckled by the mid-day sun;
> Where its slim trunk the ash from rock to rock
> Flings arching like a bridge;—that branchless ash,
> Unsunn'd and damp, whose few poor yellow leaves
> Ne'er tremble in the gale, yet tremble still
> Fann'd by the water-fall! and there my friends
> Behold the dark green file of long lank weeds,
> That all at once (a most fantastic sight!)
> Still nod and drip beneath the dripping edge
> Of the blue clay-stone.
>
> (10–20)

The remembered scene conjured up by the poet, and then imagined making its appeal to the sensibilities of others, is twice removed from simple 'descriptive painting'. Its impact is

dreamlike, strange, almost sinister, in its colouring, its secret
and ceaseless motion hidden from the light. The scene has not
only 'conversed' with Coleridge—it has haunted him and sunk
deep, so that it re-emerges like a mood of his own. It no longer
possesses an objective reality distinct from the poet's emotional
experience.

This Lime-Tree Bower deals also with the moral conversion
from sense to vision, alluding to it explicitly and also catching
the process as it takes place. Again reliving his experience by
reflecting it in another person, Coleridge evokes the state of
receptive exaltation which, though generated by response to a
landscape, comes to replace pleasure of the senses:

> So my friend
> Struck with deep joy may stand, as I have stood,
> Silent with swimming sense; yea, gazing round
> On the wide landscape, gaze till all doth seem
> Less gross than bodily; and of such hues
> As veil the Almighty Spirit, when yet he makes
> Spirits perceive his presence.

(37-43)

Nature becoming the expression of God ultimately withdraws
the beholder from the physical landscape. His 'deep joy'
translates him to a more mystical frame of mind in which all
the forms of nature are symbols pointing to a reality that over-
whelms them and renders them less clearly appreciated, because
less important, as visual phenomena. The 'gaze' takes on the
character of a spiritual communion and loses its 'grosser'
meaning as an experience of the eye. Coleridge's use of the word
'gross' here emphasizes how strongly he regards the movement
to spiritual awareness as progress towards a desirable goal, a
purified perception.

Yet, as he notes with exact eye the detail of light and shade
around him in the lime-tree bower, Coleridge restores the
balance, showing that nature seen only lazily will not allow the
revealing 'converse' with mind and feelings to begin. Sensuous
response is not to be bypassed. The poem offers us simultaneously
two stages in the process of assimilating world to mind, in that
it gives the poet's remembered and his immediate experience.
He presents the achieved vision, the landscape in terms of its

emotional life for him, and as a revelation known to his mind. He also presents the new visual encounters as they begin to work upon him and become subjectively influential, moving out of the category of objects of sense. The 'transparent foliage' of the bower, pale under the light, is noted; he watches a 'broad and sunny leaf', the shadows of 'leaf and stem' (47–50), and the changing effects of fading light on 'that walnut tree' (51), or on ivy 'which usurps Those fronting elms',

> and now, with blackest mass
> Makes their dark branches gleam a lighter hue
> Through the late twilight.
>
> (53–6)

This is the minute commentary found so often in the Notebooks, the painter's eye discerning patterns of light and registering the momentary combinations of mass and line brought about by setting sun and thickening dusk. He concentrates wholly on the particular trees and plants around him, and on the other sights and sounds of evening. But the lesson of the scene is already conditioning his response:

> No plot so narrow, be but Nature there,
> No waste so vacant, but may well employ
> Each faculty of sense, and keep the heart
> Awake to Love and Beauty!
>
> (61–4)

When the evening in the lime-tree bower becomes a remembered experience, the sensuous elements will be inseparable from the moral context and its emotions. But the poem as it stands is satisfying as a structure because it holds together the different phases in the disembodying of the physical.

The process is certainly not one of devaluation. All Coleridge's poems which display it prove the contrary: that for him, the removal of phenomena from objective independence is a proper fate, one which honours them and enables them to fulfil their true function as instruments of God and the inner life. In the first published version of *Frost at Midnight*,[50] there were several lines which show how aware he was that the 'self-watching subtilizing mind' strove always to appropriate all things to itself, as a life-giving act:

> But still the living spirit in our frame,
> That loves not to behold a lifeless thing,
> Transfuses into all its own delights,
> Its own volition.

The final text condenses this to the statement that the spirit is 'every where Echo or mirror seeking of itself' (21–2). Later in the poem he repeats once more his idea that nature is imbued with the almighty 'living spirit'. When his son is exposed to 'lakes and shores and mountain crags', he will be in contact with

> The lovely shapes and sounds intelligible
> Of that eternal language, which thy God
> Utters, who from eternity doth teach
> Himself in all, and all things in himself.
>
> (59–62)

The 'great universal Teacher' will 'mould' the spirit and 'by giving make it ask' (63–4). And 'therefore all seasons shall be sweet' (65) to the child—the chain of reasoning is emphasized by this conclusion. Not the intrinsic sensuous appeal of the 'lakes and sandy shores' (55), but the spiritual insight which is acquired by means of them: Coleridge again asserts his priorities. From all points of view, the objects of nature serve a purpose in relation to the mind, whether human or divine, and in facilitating the communion between the two.

Frost at Midnight exemplifies the relationship, and the traffic from the outer world to the inner, with absolute control of both sensuous and meditative content. Travelling through the poem, we find the journey is circular, in that it ends in the contemplation of the frost at work which was its beginning. But the detail of the 'secret ministry' is greater at the end: the 'silent icicles' have been formed, to be seen 'Quietly shining to the quiet Moon' (72–4), so that we achieve fulfilment and enlarged experience on the descriptive level. There is too a final return to the body—though this must be qualified—in a poem which throughout moves rhythmically between body and mind. Sensuous observation prompts reverie and speculation and the pattern is repeated so that there is a steady pulse of outer and inner awareness, imitating what Coleridge sees as the necessary rhythm of all creative experience. The 'thin blue flame' (13) in the grate leads into memories of school-time and its dreams of other places. Returning from this train of recollection, he watches the baby sleeping at his side, whose 'gentle breathings', audible in the deep silence, 'Fill up the interspersèd vacancies And momentary pauses of the thought!' (45–7). After this pause, and arising out of it, another meditation unfolds to draw the poem back into the mental world, a dream of a future in which Hartley will read the language of God in nature. This idea introduces the final return to specific detail of nature. Although with perfect judgment the poem comes to rest on the sensuous note which leaves it in touch with its beginning, none the less there is not simply a reversion to the body. The primacy of the inner world is maintained, for the details of robin on mossy apple-tree, the smoking thatch thawing in the sun, and the silent icicles are all dependent on the foregoing theory of God speaking through such phenomena. They end the poem, in short, as symbols, not merely as descriptive studies. Our pleasure in them should not make us isolate them, nor distract us from the concluding passage's introductory 'therefore', and the whole rhetorical structure, rounding off argument with extended example:

> Therefore all seasons shall be sweet to thee,
> Whether the summer clothe the general earth
> With greenness, or the redbreast sit and sing
> Betwixt the tufts of snow on the bare branch
> Of mossy apple-tree, while the nigh thatch
> Smokes in the sun-thaw; whether the eave-drops fall
> Heard only in the trances of the blast,
> Or if the secret ministry of frost
> Shall hang them up in silent icicles,
> Quietly shining to the quiet Moon.
>
> (65–74)

The 'secret ministry' in line one of the poem is a weather report; at its reappearance seventy-two lines later, it is a property of the poet's mind and an utterance made by God.

Such an evolution is central to Coleridge's work as a poet. In *The Nightingale* (1798), he is moved to express not merely the pleasure of listening to the bird on a particular occasion, but the import of all such experiences. Following the technique

sketched when addressing the young friend, and developed in
This Lime-Tree Bower, he exploits here the presence of several
listeners sharing the same enjoyment; and adds to the immediate
group a listener recalled from another place where nightingales
are heard. All again intensify his own response to the bird, and
help him to estimate its value to the full; a function also served
by the 'father's tale' (106) with which the poem ends. The
expectation that Hartley would enjoy the song, and the narrative of his being comforted by nature, repeat the *Frost at Midnight*
doctrine that it is wise to rear a child as 'Nature's play-mate'
(97), for the emotional and moral rewards are abundant. So
the poem, beginning with a bird singing in a quiet evening, ends
with the same bird as a symbol of a state of profound happiness.

The poem rejects the conventional idea of the nightingale as a
symbol of misery. This is an interesting qualification to Coleridge's general approval of the mind's tendency to colour all
things with itself. In a very Ruskinian passage, what he con-
demns is in effect the pathetic fallacy:

> some night-wandering man whose heart was pierced
> With the remembrance of a grievous wrong,
> Or slow distemper, or neglected love,
> (And so, poor wretch! filled all things with himself,
> And made all gentle sounds tell back the tale
> Of his own sorrow) he, and such as he,
> First named these notes a melancholy strain.
>
> (16-22)

The whole question of the pathetic fallacy will be discussed in
the following section on Ruskin, but the grounds for Coleridge's
view—and the degree to which he subscribes to it—are relevant
here. He is consistent with his much-reiterated idea of nature
as the language of God. 'In Nature there is nothing melancholy'
(15); its 'sweet voices' are 'always full of love and joyance'
(42-3), because of its office as spokesman for a supreme, bene-
ficent reality beyond itself. That is, Coleridge is not complaining
because the bird is seen in emotional terms and made subjectively
significant. On the contrary, that is to him a necessary accolade,
but it must be based on a receptive state of mind, not brought
about by the tyranny of an arbitrary mood. There is a right
and wrong way of connecting subject with object, Coleridge

45

indicates; the right way is God-given, the wrong falsifies the deepest nature of both object and subject. But such danger is not a reason for stopping short, for seeing the object only as the material for a descriptive note. The whole bias of his poems argues the other way. His ruling passion, to advance the cause of an enlightened moral and intellectual consciousness, commits him to an attack on the opacity of physical being.

The strength of Coleridge's desire to convert matter into mind is nowhere more evident than in the poem which mourns the breakdown of his power to do so. *Dejection: an Ode* (1802) brings us full circle to our starting-point in the *Biographia Literaria*, for it too sees 'objects (*as* objects) as fixed and dead', and asserts the inevitability of this unless the mind breathes into them its own vitality:

> I may not hope from outward forms to win
> The passion and the life, whose fountains are within.
>
> (45–6)

Nature can only reveal itself as the language of God if the human mind can throw around it the light which makes such a reading possible. The 'outward forms' will remain external unless the initiative can come from within to transfigure them. A passive receptivity of mind is futile—contradictory even. 'We receive but what we give' (47), and if the emotional circuit fails, the poet relapses into the unpoetic stage of registering with his senses alone: 'I see, not feel, how beautiful they are' (38). And for the object to remain an object in this way, however acutely the eye may note the sky's 'peculiar tint of yellow green' (29), is for Coleridge a disaster.

His Notebooks admit the need to give full attention to the reporting senses; they show how keen a regard he had for the detail of the universe around him. But they show too the inability of his mind to preserve distance between itself and what was noted. The move even there is towards emotional engagement and symbolic readings, the search is for 'laws' and intellectual meaning, and the instinct is to humanize what is seen. The entries are the first steps towards poetry, the preliminary studies from which the fully creative union can be developed, 'wedding Nature to us' (68). If the subjective driving-

POEMS

force dies, if the self-generated springs of joy dry up, then living contact is lost and the scrutiny of outward forms is without point or purpose. Alone they generate nothing. Poems cease, the Notebooks could only be, in their author's eye, 'fixed and dead' in their isolated observations.

Despite the gloom of the *Ode*, and the weakening of his poetic strength in later years, Coleridge did not collapse into this hopelessness. He never lost his sense of the quickening power of the mind rejoicing in itself, nor his appetite for subjective realization. His Notebooks grow, their tendencies maintained, and his theory develops along the same lines of thought. The world of sense remains vivid and real, its colours, shapes and activity of compelling interest. But its value continues to lie in its union with an inner world of whose more intangible nature it becomes eloquently expressive. 'Body is but a striving to become mind' is Coleridge's text as theorist, note-maker, and above all, as poet. He looks at his surroundings, from stones to clouds, because he wishes to discover himself.

2

RUSKIN AND 'THE PURE FACT'

RUSKIN AS POET

CONVINCED of his son's genius, John James Ruskin cherished the 'passionate hope' that he would one day write poetry 'as good as Byron's, only pious'.[1] Ruskin himself, versifying enthusiastically by the age of nine, was ready enough during his youth to share this vision of his destiny. 'J.R.' appeared frequently in *Friendship's Offering* and other annuals in the 1830s, and he competed for the Newdigate prize at Oxford three times, winning it in 1839. His feelings for Adèle Domecq and his response to his first travels abroad were all expressed in poems. Yet in 1845, when he was twenty-six, he reached the 'wholesome conclusion' as he called it that verse was not his medium and should be abandoned. 'I perceived finally that I could express nothing I had to say, rightly, in that manner.'[2] He had already written and published the first volume of *Modern Painters* by this time, and prose was to remain his medium for the rest of his life.

Ruskin's decision, the expectations which preceded it and the assumptions it involved are all important to the study of poetic directions in the mid-nineteenth century. Briefly, he reversed the movement his Romantic predecessors took for granted. Where Coleridge saw descriptive prose writing as the preliminary to poetic treatment, and in itself inferior, Ruskin found the more mature mode to be prose. Poetry for him was an inhibiting way of writing from which he had to escape in order to achieve artistic satisfaction. He was not merely rejecting verse—that is, the technical struggle with metre and rhyme—but certain assumptions which he found implicit in the idea of a poem. And these assumptions were, inevitably for one born in 1819, Romantic.

The last poems he wrote, in the early 1840s, are the ones which reveal most painfully his attempt to be an obedient

48

Romantic. They are largely inspired by his favourite Alpine region: *A Walk in Chamouni* (1843), *The Arve at Cluse* (1845), *Mont Blanc Revisited* (1845) are typical titles, and the poems show him striving to achieve the expected implications from the outer scene. A poem, that is to say, may begin by apostrophizing Mont Blanc—'Oh, mount beloved!'—but it must conclude with God. He may outline his walk and what he saw, but the poem must advance to dwell on the 'deep stillness of Omnipotence', advertising, that is, the results of the experience, and stressing this rather than the sensuous response. The rushing Arve becomes a human mirror; it flows 'perplexed and pale', its restlessness is 'unprofitable' and it displays the moral shortcomings of the poet who watches it, 'proud, impatient and pollute!'

Ruskin in these poems is following the creed of humanization. 'Colouring . . . the landscape with reflections from human life'[3] was not of course altogether alien to his nature, and its place in his prose will be discussed later. But the poems only strain to bring about the transmutation from fact to feeling, from things seen to moral interpretation. There is none of Coleridge's confidence in the destined union between subject and object, no instantaneous conversion of the 'external real' into the inner world. His poems lack the spark which in the best Romantic work kindles the one flame. He transfers attention from the scene to the observer not by the fluent handling of imaginative relationships but by rhetorical emotion and platitudinous moral statement. 'So stands the Providence of God' he announces, having contemplated Mont Blanc. Leaving what he sees, he becomes grandiose, his words signifying not a development of insight but a failure to effect the change to new vision. He offers piety but not poetry.

His dissatisfaction with himself as a poet comes to a head in the works where he has tried most deliberately to let the humanizing tendency dominate and direct the style and structure. If we compare the work of this period with earlier efforts, in particular with the most spontaneous verses of his boyhood, we begin to see that in certain ways, such a tendency was uncongenial to him. Other characteristics were strongly inbred and they ensured that the Romantic bias towards subjective

49

emphasis was, at least, tempered with contrary instincts and, at most, aroused his outright hostility.

As his editors say in their Introduction to the poems, 'his . . . eyes were fixed on nature before he was in his teens'.[4] At eight years of age, he reported to his father his experiences at Glenfarg in Scotland:

> Papa, how pretty those icicles are . . .
> And mountains at a distance seen,
> And rivers winding through the plain;
> And quarries with their craggy stones.

The *Iteriad* of a Lakes tour (1830–1) manages to combine doggerel narrative with accurate descriptive detail: 'A ridge we beheld ('twas of loose slaty stone)', and in 1829 he matches observation with drama in a title—*On the Appearance of a Sudden Cloud of Yellow Fog Covering Everything with Darkness*. At Walter Scott's grave in 1832 he reveals his taste for exactness:

> The river rolls clear over pebble and weed;
> The wave is bright, and the foam is light,
> All in the eddies gurgling white . . .

Fresh description continues to be a salient mark of the poems into the mid-1830s, as his *Account of a Tour on the Continent* (1833–4) shows. Coblenz is neatly characterized, 'the tall red roofs, the long white bridge', and the source of the Arveron in its mixture of water and light: 'chasms of paly green The shivery sunshine shot between'. There is a naïve immediacy of place and weather:

> oh, we are on the mountain-top!
> The clouds float by in fleecy flock,
> Heavy, and dank.

More prolonged sky study is recorded in a verse letter to his father in 1835:

> This evening, ere the night closed in,
> I was admiring of the sky.
> Clouds, grey and colourless and thin,
> Were scattered everywhere on high;
> But o'er the Norwood hills did lie
> A heap of cold unbroken white.

These extracts are sufficient to establish that young Ruskin wished his poetic utterances to fix, as an important part of their purpose, his sensuous experience of landscape and sky. To understand the extent of his commitment to such records, we must take into account other pursuits and other writings of his earlier days. A pointer is given in the poem called *A Tour through France to Chamouni* (1835) which attempts a Byronic jauntiness but includes a survey of geological theories of the flood, ending with the imagined vision of the geologist:

> Before him solid mountains wave and twist,
> And forms of life within them fossilize;
> The flint invades each member as it dies,
> And through the quivering corse on creeps the stone,
> Till in the mountain's hardened heart it lies,
> In nature, rock,—in form, a skeleton.

He dismisses the idea: 'Thus on Jura dreamed I, with nice touch Discriminating stones'. He could not have described himself more truly. From his infancy Ruskin was happy when 'discriminating stones' and acquiring geological data. His mineral collections began on the journeys of his childhood and, as he recalls in *Praeterita*, the 'most exciting event' on first climbing Snowdon was finding 'a piece of copper pyrites'. But he adds: 'the general impression of Welsh mountain form was so true and clear that subsequent journeys little changed or deepened it'.[5] He saw the mineral detail and the larger aspect of the place with equal acuteness. Also, his powers of observation can already be discerned here as being partly scientific and partly an artistic grasp of form and appearance. As his tastes developed, the two became consciously distinguished, though never separated; and *Praeterita* insists first of all on the undisputed primacy of the sense of sight in his childhood, the 'habit of fixed attention'[6] as it grew upon him. He looked at 'the sky, the leaves, and pebbles',[7] and 'was only interested by things near' him, or 'at least clearly visible and present'.[8] He thinks his intense study of objects unique: 'I have never known [a child] whose thirst for visible fact was at once so eager and so methodic';[9] and he regards the absence of self-awareness as being one of the pleasures of this cast of mind. All his concentration was exercised on the world around, and his own place in the scene was irrelevant: 'my entire delight was in observing without being myself noticed,—if I could have been invisible, all the better'. Personal anonymity was and has remained a key part of 'the essential love *of Nature*',[10] he asserts.

Certainly the instinctive habits of the child were never renounced. As soon as he began to keep diaries, they became repositories for all that was harvested by the 'eager and methodic' observer. From 1835, geological, botanical, meteorological and simply visual notes give them their character. One entry, that of 18 May 1842, may be taken as typical:

read chemistry and draw leaves. A fine bit of sunset . . . clouds in swift motion revealing red masses of cumuli behind, seen against green open sky.[11]

The immediate outlet for the kind of material accumulated in the diaries took the form of scientific articles. He was to draw on it later in his work for *Modern Painters* and other prose. But in the first instance it lent itself more readily to be turned into contributions to Loudon's *Magazine of Natural History* than into poems for *Friendship's Offering*. This is a point of some significance in relation to his withdrawal from poetry. Cook and Wedderburn in their introduction to the articles remark that 'they are interesting as showing his close observation, and the analytic turn of his mind'.[12] The first one, appearing in 1834, was Ruskin's first published work and was called, 'Enquiries on the Cause of the Colour of the Water of the Rhine', a title which itself points to the author's ability to combine a responsive eye with the impulse to investigate. He values phenomena in both ways, with no sense of conflict, because to him each kind of observation and study increases his appreciative understanding of what he sees. Both focus attention sharply on the natural object and to Ruskin it deserves no less. A profound respect for the external world unifies his contemplation of its colours, forms and qualities. In another article of the same year, 'Facts and Considerations on the Strata of Mont Blanc; and on some instances of twisted Strata observable in Switzerland', he claims simply that 'the granite ranges of Mont Blanc are as interesting to the geologist as they are to the painter'.[13] He looks at the mountains—or individual stones—with the eyes of both, while his botanical notes and sketches cannot be segregated from those drawings which record his love for the flower as it grows.

Such concentration on the features of the earth, involving both a curiosity about appearance and structure and an aesthetic admiration for objects of nature, either singly or as composite scenes, was not peculiar to Ruskin in this period of the nineteenth century. From childhood it ruled him with particular strength, but the trend of the time roughly from 1820 to 1850 was in general sympathy with his devotion to fact. The history of the various editions of Wordsworth's *Guide to the Lakes* is relevant here. Having begun its career in 1810 as an introduction to a set of undistinguished drawings of the Lakes, it lost these in 1820 in favour of the author's poems. But in 1822 it was published on its own, a descriptive guide accepted without other aids or associations. Then in the editions of 1842 and 1853 there were added what W. M. Merchant calls 'a mass of technical accretions'.[14] 'Outline diagrams' of the mountains replaced the picturesque engravings of thirty years before and where once Wordsworth's poems had appeared stood lists of plants and shells connected with the area, and 'Letters on the Geology of the Lake District' by Professor Sedgwick. These later editions enjoyed very large sales.

The enthusiasm for fact adumbrated in the fortunes of the *Guide* is supported by other evidence, from both arts and sciences. The energies of the latter especially during the 1830s were largely devoted to the collection, classification and close scrutiny of phenomena. As Henry Ladd says,[15] it was a science concerned with detail—animal, mineral and vegetable—and Ruskin's taste for descriptive analysis was fostered by it. He met Sedgwick and was taught by William Buckland, geologist and churchman, at Oxford. The 'half-theological' aspect of this science was a further recommendation,[16] but its passion for fact, for the thing seen and handled, was its primary attraction for Ruskin, as for the many amateur scientists whose enthusiastic presence is vouched for by such magazines as Loudon's.

In the arts, 'the first half of the nineteenth century was the golden age of the English illustrated travel book or book of views'.[17] And, as Wordsworth's *Guide* shows, the trend of taste was away from picturesque scenic arrangements, either verbal

53

or painted, towards a greater factual, informative accuracy. Descriptive writing flourished, but travel books had to convince their readers that they were receiving an impression of the real thing, the place as it actually appeared. Illustrators or 'topographers' had to work to the same standard. Ladd remarks:

> However brilliant their poetical effects of light, atmosphere and storm clouds, however subtle the compositions they devised, there was always the understanding on the part of their public that a picture was a picture of a certain place and, even more important, that this was the way that place or that tree or that castle looked.[18]

It is not surprising, then, that Ruskin's equipment for his travels to Switzerland in 1835 should include a 'cyanometer' to measure the blue of the sky, a notebook for geological observations and sketchblock, square rule and foot-rule for architectural drawings. At the same time it was also his intention to make a poetic record of the journey, a kind of *Don Juan* blended with *Childe Harold*.[19] In the event, the notebooks and perhaps the cyanometer were more diligently exercised than his poetic faculties, which began with bravura but had exhausted their superlatives before the Alps were reached. We return, therefore, to the problems of Ruskin as poet.

His childhood saw no difficulty. He read 'Joyce's Scientific Dialogues' and *Manfred* with equal zest and drew on each for his effort at story-telling when he was seven. His poems at the same age range in subject from 'the Steam-engine' to 'the Rainbow',[20] and in the other examples quoted earlier his appetite for 'visible fact' is not thwarted or inhibited by verse composition. But as he gets older the double role of nature observer and poet proves harder to sustain. The passion for studying phenomena grew steadily, the desire to produce poetic masterpieces was still felt, but by the early 1840s an incompatibility in these aims can be discerned. The painful awakening and frustration of his emotional life in relation to Adèle Domecq no doubt played its part in opening up divisions in his mind. His decision in March 1840 to split his diary into two sections, one for 'feeling' and one for 'intellect',[21] coincides with Adèle's wedding, but it is a notion of more extensive significance.

Coleridge could never have conceived any such division in his notebooks. To him, intellect and feeling were collaborating in the exploration of the self and external phenomena. Together they revealed the relationships binding the universe in a profound unity. And for him, the poetic act is precisely that which unites fact, thought and feeling. Ruskin, inheriting the simplified assumption that poetry rates feeling and idea higher than fact, tries in his adult poems to achieve that weighting. Yet his instincts oppose the effort. He wishes to dwell on fact, to exhibit and study it, not relegate it to a supporting role. The swift transition from the physical to the psychological is a development he is reluctant to admit and he does not see the world of feeling as an enriching context, but rather as a hindrance to the due honouring of phenomena as such. The proper tribute in Ruskin's view is not possible if the observer is more concerned with his reacting self, his emotional response, or with any other centre which seems to deprive the object of the full attention it merits in its independent existence.

It becomes apparent in the early 1840s, therefore, that Ruskin must either continue to accept the Romantic subjective view of poetry, and cease to write it, or he must reject that approach and establish the right of fact to a primary place in poems. What he actually does is not so clear-cut, but is the more interesting for that. He makes no absolute choice but contrives to move in both directions in such a way that he achieves the maximum propaganda for 'pure fact'. That is, in practice he accepts the Romantic position by abandoning poetry and keeping Coleridge's allocation of the world of sense to 'descriptive tour' prose. But the prose of *Modern Painters* enthrones the world of nature in all its colour and detail with such energy of presentation that it amounts to a revaluation of descriptive writing. What to Coleridge was material for the notebook or the humbler travel narrative is transformed into an artistic achievement which refuses to remain demoted to a secondary, or preliminary, category. And in his theory, later in *Modern Painters*, Ruskin takes also the alternative course of denying poetry's bias towards the subjective. He argues that the greatest poetic work is marked by an impersonal quality, by its ability to see clearly with no confusion of emotion and object and no

55

Arnold's views.

imposition of self on scene or situation. The 'pathetic fallacy' is the term in which he sums up his point of view.

Before going on to consider, first the theory of *Modern Painters* and secondly the descriptive art of Ruskin, I want to look a little more closely at the crucial year 1842, the 'birth-year'[22] in which his future course was revealed to him and in which he gave up his attempts to be a Romantic poet.

The eagerness to grasp place or object exactly as it looked is marked in 1841, when his architectural sketches were drawn, he says, 'with an acuteness of delight in the thing as it actually stood'. The result was both 'living and like',[23] and his *Modern Painters* criteria for art are laid down both in the delight and the judgment. But in the next year two experiences dramatized his mounting enthusiasm for 'that place' and 'that tree'. He describes in *Praeterita* first, how a 'bit of ivy' brought him to a moment of revelation:

one day on the road to Norwood, I noticed a bit of ivy round a thorn stem . . . and proceeded to make a light and shade pencil study of it in my grey paper pocket-book, carefully, as if it had been a bit of sculpture, liking it more and more as I drew. When it was done, I saw that I had virtually lost all my time since I was twelve years old, because no one had ever told me to draw what was really there![24]

And later, at Fontainebleau, he found his view confined one day to 'that small aspen tree against the blue sky':

Languidly, but not idly, I began to draw it; and as I drew, the languor passed away: the beautiful lines insisted on being traced,— without weariness. More and more beautiful they became, as each rose out of the rest, and took its place in the air. With wonder increasing every instant, I saw that they 'composed' themselves, by finer laws than any known of men. At last, the tree was there, and everything that I had thought before about trees, nowhere . . . that all the trees of the wood (for I saw surely that my little aspen was only one of their millions) should be beautiful . . . this was indeed an end to all former thoughts with me, an insight into a new silvan world.[25]

He goes on to speak of 'the bond between the human mind and all visible things' in terms of a revelation of divine laws. Van

Akin Burd[26] challenges *Praeterita*'s fidelity to memory on this point when he compares its recollections of 1842 with the actual diary record for the year, which Ruskin was not able to consult when he reconstructed it for the memoir. Burd argues that old Ruskin misrepresents his youthful excitement by making his aspen experience—absent altogether from the diary—'almost mystic'. Where *Praeterita* suggests that 1842 brought 'the awakening of a kind of Wordsworthian insight', the diary 'shows Ruskin preoccupied with an objective study of the beautiful forms which he had learned to see in nature'. To my mind, *Praeterita* does not contradict the evidence of the diary, because it makes clear that any discovery of 'laws' in the universe was only arrived at by the development of close study of natural detail. The laws are not beyond or behind the facts but within them. Religious emotion may well have been generated; the diary never set out to expand on such insights in the *Praeterita* manner. But in both accounts, the immediate and the recollected, Ruskin's learning to see 'what was really there', his sudden illuminated reading of the lines of the aspen until it 'was there' on his paper: these are the prophetic events. As Burd says, the diary of 1842 shows him exercising his 'remarkable curiosity', pursuing the truth and beauty of fact by means of 'the most objective kind of observation'. He was working 'almost with the eye of a prospective botanist or geologist', and awakening to the 'beauty of form' by this minute scrutiny. The impulse to embark on such a work as *Modern Painters* may not be mentioned, but it was prompted by these movements of his mind and the ever more concentrated attention he was paying to the world of visible fact. His earliest instincts were coming fully into their own. By 1844 he 'had learned to draw . . . with great botanical precision'. That is, he had learned to see not passively but with an unremitting energy of the eye, and in consequence he was 'interested in everything, from clouds to lichens'.[27]

And, in consequence also, he was less interested in his poems. His impatience shows itself in a letter he wrote at Chamouni to W. H. Harrison in June 1842. 'Every moment of time is so valuable—between mineralogy and drawing—and getting ideas', he reports, and goes on:

for not an hour, from dawn to moonrise, on any day since I have been in sight of Mont Blanc has passed without its own peculiar—unreportable—evanescent phenomena, that I can hardly prevail upon myself to snatch a moment for work on verses which I feel persuaded I shall in a year or two almost entirely re-write.[28]

Working on poems, moving away from the fact to the feeling, is but a feeble rival to the excitements of the world around. He is 'so occupied in the morning—and so tired at night—with snow and granite' that nothing else matters. The 'pure facts' command his allegiance, not as phenomena in need of humanization, but as snow, granite, aspen trees and bits of ivy. Not Manfred's agonies, but the stones and strata of the mountain on which he stands, now call to Ruskin for recognition. And he turns to a kind of writing, as well as drawing, in which they can receive a full acknowledgment.

The child who would never have written sonnets to the celandine 'because it is of a coarse, yellow and imperfect form'[29] was the father of the man who in 1842 fully found himself. The 'plain and leafy fact'[30] of the primrose was to be studied, if the flower were ever to become eloquent to him; he had no desire that a daisy might admire its own shadow, but devoted his attention 'to trying to draw the shadow rightly' himself. The boy and the man alike honour the world they see, and in the volumes of *Modern Painters* from 1843 to 1860, this acuteness of eye found its proper expression.

Ruskin was not content merely to find a verbal form in which he could communicate the richness of an objective vision. He wished also to establish a theory of art in which such a vision should appear pre-eminent, and could be argued as a key to artistic quality, whether pictorial or verbal. The work of Turner gave him his opportunity, on the one hand, to exalt the pure fact into an artistic principle and, on the other, to create his own verbal art of descriptive prose. Ruskin's view of Turner and his role as the painter's champion will therefore provide the basis for a discussion of the general theory of *Modern Painters*, seen in relation to the specifically literary theory in Volume III, turning on the pathetic fallacy.

THE PATHETIC FALLACY

(i) *Context: Turner and 'Modern Painters'*

In the *Biographia Literaria* Coleridge lashed the reviewers of his day for their unworthy practices. He attacked their tendency to substitute 'assertion for argument' and the frequency of 'arbitrary and sometimes petulant verdicts'. Citing the abuse suffered by Wordsworth, he concludes that judgments so obviously warped 'prove nothing but the pitiable state of the critic's own taste and sensibility'.[31] One of the prime motives of the *Biographia*, in fact, is to establish sound principles for criticism, a purpose which leads Coleridge on to examine the nature of imagination itself. From the examination, Wordsworth emerges as an exemplar of true imaginative power.

In *Modern Painters* Ruskin produces a mid-century *Biographia*, for he too is impelled by a fierce indignation against the iniquities of reviewers, particularly when they are faced with genius they fail to comprehend. And he too is driven to a full-scale investigation of imaginative principles as a context for his evaluation of the artist whom he regards as supreme in his time. Turner is his hero, and the change of medium indicates some new assumptions and expectations. Where Coleridge's argument moves ever deeper into metaphysics, Ruskin's chosen ground is the science of aspects and appearances. But their desire to promote the proper understanding of the misunderstood works of original genius, and the ardour with which the mission is undertaken, unites them. Both the early and the mid-nineteenth century produce champions of formidable presence to fight for the art of each period which is known by all to be distinctive, and believed by the few to be great. Each defence stands as a document testifying to and helping to establish the artistic criteria of its period.

Ruskin's 'black anger' against Turner's detractors first found written expression in 1836, when he dashed off a reply to an abusive article in *Blackwood's Magazine*. The 'Mercury and Argus', currently exhibited at the Royal Academy, was dismissed as 'all blood and chalk' and the artist derided for his inability to see nature properly:

59

Whenever Nature ... shall make ... this green earth to alternate
between brimstone and white, set off with brightest blues that no
longer shall keep their distance; when cows shall be made of white
paper ... and when human eyes shall be happily gifted with a
kaleidoscopic power to patternize all confusion ... then will Turner
be a greater painter than ever the world yet saw, or than ever the
world, constituted as it is at present, wishes to see.[32]

Ruskin's line of defence was to maintain that Turner's nature
should be acceptable to the world as it is. Although his article
was unpublished, it demonstrates the weapons he would choose
to fight with seven years later, when *Modern Painters* began his
public campaign.

Since most of the attacks on Turner continued to be centred on
his supposed inability to paint recognizable versions of nature,
it was not surprising that one who admired his work should base
his arguments on the same ground and steadily seek to refute
the charges of infidelity to the natural scene. Other kinds of
defence might have been more rewarding—or so twentieth-
century art criticism is disposed to argue—but to the early
Victorian the criterion of accurate visual perception was
paramount, encouraged in art and science alike. As I have
already suggested, Ruskin belonged to his age in this respect,
and in addition his personal faculties of perception were
developing acutely in the 1836–42 period, together with his
feeling for Turner's art. The two enthusiasms grew, not only
simultaneously, but in close collaboration: the more he studied
the world of granite and snow, clouds and lichens, the more
he was convinced of Turner's power. What he looked at so
scrupulously himself, he realized Turner had seen with clarity
also. Nature and Turner's pictures confirmed each other to
Ruskin's eye. His diaries in 1841 display the intimate association
always ready in his mind.

On an Italian journey he notes of the scenery near Naples
that 'it was a Turner';[33] and of the sea, 'with the infinite
delicacy of multitudinous touches of light', he observes that one
cannot look at it 'without remembering Turner'.[34] A view along
the road makes him 'quite sick with delight', and it is 'as bright
as a first-rate Turner'.[35] Nature can surpass the painter—the
light in St Mark's square on 12 May is 'such as Turner in his

maddest moments never came up to'[36]—but the effects of nature and his art are always comparable to Ruskin's responsive gaze. The sky shows 'Turner clouds',[37] or 'minute Turner detail in subdued white and melting blue',[38] and flashes of lightning are 'Turner's own'.[39]

He never forgets the painter, and nature makes it impossible for him to do so. The more keenly he teaches himself to see the natural world, the more Turner's art is revealed to him, and the more deeply he reads Turner's pictures, the more nature's subtleties of light, form and texture become apparent. In the critics' persistent attacks at each Academy showing of Turner's work, therefore, Ruskin felt the insults with double force: his admiration for the paintings was outraged, but so too was his passion for the nature they were said to distort. To Ruskin the critics were blasphemously ignorant of nature as well as art. Both his gods were mocked in their diatribes, as when *The Times* in 1841 could claim that the latest Turner represented 'nothing in nature beyond eggs and spinach', and *The Athenaeum* could dismiss 'Glaucus and Scylla' as 'the fruits of a diseased eye and a reckless hand'.[40] The disease and the recklessness were to him only in the reviewers, unable to see what was before them either on a canvas or in the world around.

Further 'unmeasured vapid abuse'[41] in 1842 brought him to the pitch of resolution. Turner must be 'praised rightly'[42] and rescued from the heavy mockeries of critics who assert that he paints with 'yolk of egg, or currant jelly' and a 'whole array of kitchen stuff', or state bluntly that 'neither by land or water was such a scene ever witnessed' as the 'Snow-Storm'.[43] The latter was the accusation he resented most and he wrote *Modern Painters* on behalf of snow-storms, as well as in ardent support of Turner's portrayal of them. When he recalls the 'birth-year' of 1842 in the Epilogue of *Modern Painters* III, he links his 'mountain-studies and geological researches' with his feeling for Turner at the time and suggests that the zest with which he embarked on *Modern Painters* was the product of his joint devotion to the painter and the painter's subjects. He wrote the first volume in the grip of the discovery that the two were united in his mind and that in defending Turner he was celebrating nature as he could never freely do in his poems. 'In the full enthusiasm and rush of sap in the too literally sapling and stripling mind of me',[44] as he says, he brought together not only art and nature, but his scientific and literary instincts as well. In the mission of proving Turner's truth to nature he found a way of fulfilling his strong need to concentrate on sensory perception and the study of the object. The extension of the work into five volumes over a period of seventeen years may blur some of his argument and lead to intellectual entanglements which confuse most readers and scandalize philosophers, but the distinctive union of forces and interests in Ruskin's mind persists throughout the books. To the end *Modern Painters* upholds the place of fact, especially natural fact, in art, and the duty of the artist to respect it totally. What he has to say about beauty and imagination is grounded in the honouring of fact, and in its promotion to the status of a primary creative concept lies one of the main contrasts with the *Biographia Literaria*. As A. H. Warren says: 'Ruskin preached the exact representation of facts or truths of nature without generalization or selection, and without the intrusion of arbitrary moral or emotional peculiarities that belong to the artistic temperament. Truth is the object of art, and only so much beauty is allowed in the representation as is consistent with truth.'[45] Art, in short, 'must always give facts' and 'artistic truth is first of all truth of sense impression'.[46]

The Preface to the second edition of *Modern Painters* I establishes his terms of argument with all the vigour of his 'stripling' mind, but they remain valid for the volumes written when the sap rose less freely. He states his aims with regard to Turner most succinctly in the final paragraph:

For many a year we have heard nothing with respect to the works of Turner but accusations of their want of *truth*. To every observation on their power, sublimity, or beauty, there has been but one reply: they are not like nature. I therefore took my opponents on their own ground, and demonstrated, by thorough investigation of actual facts, that Turner *is* like nature, and paints more of nature than any man who ever lived.[47]

The extravagance of the claim in the last sentence is typical of the tone of the 1843 volume, where all landscape painters except

Turner are dismissed with asperity or at the most with grudging and extremely qualified praise. Testing them always by the experience of his own senses, he finds them wanting: they are not like nature. And though in later years he was ready to admit that some of his judgments were presumptuous, the result of youthful ignorance, he never relinquishes the standard by which he awards or withholds his admiration. In 1854, two years before he added Volume III, he notes in his Paris diary:

The grand impression on me, in walking through Louvre after Switzerland, is the utter *coarseness* of painting, especially as regards mountains. The universal principle of blue mass behind and green or brown banks or bushes in front. No real sense of height or distance, no care, no detail, no affection. To think of the soft purple dawns melting along the heights of the Valais—and then of such things as these! [48]

And in 1856 he notes that while at Dover he 'ascertained Turner's singular veracity in the way the waves threw up . . . pieces of timber'. [49]

'Singular veracity' is the great example set by Turner in Ruskin's eyes. Art, he insists, is concerned with the 'loving study of nature as she is' [50] and he attacks the neglect of 'specific form' in favour of a more idealized presentation of general truths, or some idiosyncratic treatment of forms which draws attention to the artist rather than the subject. The 'violation of natural distinctions' is painting's deadly sin, and fidelity to individual detail is as right for the inanimate aspects of nature as it is for the living: 'it is just as impossible to generalize granite and slate, as it is to generalize a man and a cow'. The highest landscape painting, in short, is that which is based on 'perfect cognizance of the form, functions, and system of every organic or definitely structured existence which it has to represent'. [51] The painter must achieve the accuracy of zoologist, geologist, botanist and meteorologist, although he is not pursuing the same end as these scientists.

What Ruskin advocates in painters and their audience alike is first of all the full development of the faculty of sight. Our failure is never to see clearly: 'men usually see little of what is before their eyes'. [52] A vague and misty sense of nature is to be deplored because it weakens art, handicaps assessment of artists, and, further, is a deficiency affecting our moral and emotional lives, our whole scale of values. *Modern Painters* pursues the issues of aesthetic judgments and moral insights, but it insists on the fundamental importance of a real, discriminating and complete encounter with natural phenomena as the way to such perceptions. A mere acquaintance with clouds, water, or leaves is an inadequate preparation for valuable painting or valuable living. Constantly throughout the volumes, Ruskin emphasizes Turner's ability to see more, and more thoroughly, than other artists.

He is 'the only perfect landscape painter', the only one 'who has ever given an entire transcript of the whole system of nature'.[53] Each cloud he executes is 'a picture in itself'; he knows and shows our lazy eyes that no cloud is 'in the least like another',[54] or that 'there is not a leaf in the world which has the *same colour* visible over its whole surface'.[55] Only Turner has seen nature, from a stone to a mountain, in the fullest way: he is 'as much of a geologist as he is of a painter'[56] and he demands from us a similar degree of attentive regard—'we see the absolute necessity of scientific and entire acquaintance with nature, before this great artist can be understood'.[57] Yet though the energy of his vision rivals and includes the scientist's careful scrutiny, it is not directed to analytical ends nor based on specialized intellectual study of his subjects.

Turner's greatness and rightness in all these points . . . depend on no scientific knowledge . . . He had merely accustomed himself to see impartially, intensely, and fearlessly.[58]

The science of which he is the master is not that of the microscope or the test tube, but the 'science of aspects',[59] the lively perception of phenomena in their intimate detail as vital parts of nature's landscape: the flower as it grows, the rock as it rests, the cloud as it moves. Such a science of the visual sense necessarily includes an emotional response, unlike analytical research, Ruskin argues. In further hyperbole, he calls Turner, 'the first poet who has, in all their range, understood the grounds of noble emotion which exist in landscape'.

The phrase 'noble emotion' implies the inevitable connection in Ruskin's mind between the feelings and the moral life. But before I move into this area of his argument, it is important to emphasize again that the achievement of 'impartial, intense and fearless' seeing is for him the prime qualification of the great artist. Emotion and further enlightenment depend upon the completeness of the encounter with the object. If it is only vaguely seen, manipulated for the artist's convenience, or reduced to his preconceived assumptions about it, there will be no revelation, no noble emotion. Turner is to be acknowledged as a hyper-sensitive eye before he can be hailed as nature's interpreter. That role arises out of his subjection to the snow-storm, the cloud or the sea; he does not begin from his emotions about these things. The facts come first.

Indeed, the more facts an artist offers, the greater he is, Ruskin claims in *Modern Painters*.[60] Such a pronouncement sounds less crude as we begin to recognize that being able to see the facts of nature is for Ruskin not in the least a routine or automatic activity, but rather, a rare gift and hence a mark of genius. He is not reducing art to proficient copying, and his criteria are not those of the public seeking in an approximate, superficial way to identify a picture with its subject. He defends Turner's adaptations or adjustments of landscape features as an authentic device aiding the painter in his attempt to capture the true character of place. Such selection is the legitimate work of the 'associative' imagination. The sacredness of fact does not involve slavish obedience to exact topography. It lies elsewhere, being apparent only to those capable of the 'perfect cognizance of the form, functions, and system of every organic or definitely structured existence'. As Cook sums it up, to Ruskin 'a painter may or may not be justified in moving a tree from this place to that; he cannot be justified in making an oak move like "indiarubber"'.[61] Seeing, that is, does not consist of a comparatively passive observation of what things look like: it demands a much more strenuous effort of perception from the observer. Turner, says his champion, not only registered the appearance of mountains, water or trees: he 'learned their organisation'.[62]

The phrase is a key one if we want to grasp fully what Ruskin means by his insistence on artistic truth to nature and the supremacy of fact. The sections of *Modern Painters* to which he gives such titles as 'Of Truth of Skies', 'Of Truth of Water', 'Of Mountain Beauty', 'Of Leaf Beauty', include many passages illustrating how central to his sense of visual fact is the perception of structural qualities. Drawing mountain form is very difficult, he observes in Volume IV, and success depends on a grasp of the laws of a mountain's construction, not merely an acquaintance with its general shape and dimensions. It has to be read more closely, the artist learning to see it in terms of its fundamental being: as he 'increases in acuteness of perception, the facts which *become* outward and apparent to him are those which bear upon the growth or make of the thing'.[63] This is the goal, to see not merely what 'the thing' looks like, but to perceive the laws of its structure, how it comes to be itself. To Ruskin, if the visual sense is keen enough to achieve such insight into the nature of the object it is a creative power, and whatever the philosophic weaknesses and intellectual equivocation in the arguments used in *Modern Painters*, this remains a point consistently held and persistently demonstrated throughout.

He urges on the artist a kind of magnifying-glass concentration, so that by scrutinizing each stone and each patch of earth he may recognize not only their particular character but the connections which hold good in the physical universe. 'A stone . . . will be found a mountain in miniature',[64] the curves of a waterfall and those of a bird's feathers are related, and there is a structural bond 'between the smallest eminences and the highest'.[65] The artist should be ready to study 'among the grass and weeds', learning to trace in the soil itself 'the delicate fissure, and descending curve, and undulating shadow,' for 'he who cannot make a bank sublime will make a mountain ridiculous'.[66] On the larger scale, in a range of mountains, to the seeing eye there is no confusion or discord, but 'a great and harmonious whole', a sense of 'unity and connection' among the variety of the peaks.[67] Good and intelligent mountain-drawing is to be distinguished from bad by its ability to convey such a vision of 'some great harmony among the summits'.[68]

The last phrase, like the other observations about mountains, might have been written by Coleridge. So too might a report on the appearance of a swift-flowing stream:

66

the most exquisite arrangements of curved lines, perpetually changing from convex to concave and *vice versa*, following every swell and hollow of the bed with their modulating grace, and all in unison of motion . . .[69]

Ruskin's sense of unity amid diversity is akin to Coleridge's dominant perception, and he maintains similarly that it is a property of the imagination. But in his awareness of the structural properties which make up 'the fact' of an object of nature and in his alertness to affinities between large and small, the relation of the miniature to the grand, he changes the emphasis. The connecting of parts to make a unified whole is to Ruskin more of a literal than a philosophic idea. He approaches what he calls 'organization' with the expectation of a scientist; that is, he expects to discover the structure of an object, or of a group of objects, by observation. Creativity lies for him in the insights won by 'eager watchfulness'. His aim is the ever-increasing revelation of the phenomena of the physical universe as the eye learns to read them: the art and the science of aspects, in short. Coleridge, on the other hand, though he too sees acutely, deduces more from his observations, treating them as stimuli to a 'dance of thought'. Phenomena to him as we saw, are symbols rather than facts, and they excite him for this reason. He finds mirrors in the world of nature for his intuitions, theories and beliefs. The relationship of parts to wholes, the organization of things, are not to him important for the light they shed on the full character of the objects in themselves; he does not seek to experience the sensory fact ever more completely. Ruskin, however, is at the service of the fact in the intensity of his desire to know the object: his mind and his visual experience coincide in a single ambition. Henry Ladd, referring to the metaphysics of self-consciousness in God and man so central to the *Biographia*'s approach to the imagination, asserts bluntly that 'none of this kind of speculation ever entered Ruskin's head; his writing is in no sense metaphysical, nor does his theory confer on the imagination an intellectual function'. His ideal artist is one who 'perceives nature as a naturalist, naïvely, with no subtle inner involution of "subject or object"'.[70]

Ruskin's tree studies demonstrate particularly clearly the degree to which he transfers attention to the thing seen and his striving to reach that revelation of its nature which he holds to be inherent in its structural laws. As in the encounter with the aspen in 1842, these laws must be divined not by botanical methods of technical analysis but by the sensitive eye apprehending the growing form:

there is that about the growing of the tree trunk, and that grace in its upper ramification, which cannot be taught, and which cannot even be seen but by eager watchfulness.[71]

And:

I find there is quite an infinite interest in watching the different ways in which trees part their sprays . . . and the sometimes abrupt, sometimes gentle and undiscoverable, severing of the upright stem into the wandering and wilful branches . . .[72]

To a discerning scrutiny the tree will reveal the secrets of its laws through every detail of its organization. Leaves as they grow have their structural relationships as well as trunk and branches:

any group of four or five leaves, presenting itself in its natural position to the eye, consists of a series of forms connected by exquisite and complex symmetries . . .[73]

These 'subtle conditions of form'[74] delight Ruskin wherever he perceives them, and prominent in his visual experience is his appreciation of formal qualities in relation to the whole life of the tree. And for him, if nature is not growing, it is animated by motion, as clouds or rivers, or it seems, however solidly immobile, to incorporate the expression of movement in its structure. If there is a 'current of life and motion' in 'every fibre'[75] of a tree, there is an 'eternal changefulness'[76] in water. The 'energy and elasticity'[77] of the limbs of a tree are matched by the energy implied by the line and thrust of mountain formation:[78]

while the main energy of the mountain mass tosses itself against the central chain of Mont Blanc . . . it is met by a group of counter-crests, like the recoil of a broken wave cast against it from the other side; and yet, as the recoiling water has a sympathy with the under-swell of the very wave against which it clashes, the whole mass writhes together in strange unity of mountain passion.[79]

Turner is praised for his ability to show the 'palpitating, perpetual change' in nature and especially for his power to convey the quality of light: the 'living light', which can absorb, or is 'glowing, or flashing, or scintillating, according to what it strikes'.[80]

So there are, it emerges, several facets to Ruskin's exaltation of fact and the capacity to see it. His central lament is that 'we never see anything clearly',[81] but what he means by accuracy of perception is not as simple as we might assume. Full sensory recognition of the object involves us intimately with its structural laws: we must 'learn its organization' as well as grasp its outlines. And, as an integral feature of such organization, we must recognize the dynamic qualities of what we see, whether this be a question of organic life, the vitality of motion or the power frozen within massive form. Moreover, being aware of nature's energies includes discerning change in the sense of historical processes, the passing of time and its effects. Ruskin's descriptive passages frequently exhibit his temporal concern with his subject, alluding to past formative periods and a future of maturity or dissolution, whether of rocks or rain-showers. That he takes such data as evidence of seeing clearly what is visible at a particular moment is made explicit at the beginning of *Modern Painters*. Here he insists that when the facts which really matter are identified they will be those communicating both what has been and what is to be, as well as the present character of the object. Seeing clearly, in other words, means reading deeply into the object, recognizing the comprehensiveness of its self-expression, as it demonstrates its energies, displays the formal laws of its being, and sums up its past and its potential simply by the impact of its visual presence.

Although it insists on the need to regard fact highly, *Modern Painters* is no Gradgrind manual. Ruskin values facts for their eloquence, their revelatory character. Properly known and respected, they renew the universe for us; once we see clearly, the dull and blurred appearances of the natural world are restored to their original sharpness, variety and individuality. The personality of objects is discovered. And only from the closest study of the distinctive self of each tree or stone or cloud can we approach nature's ruling concept of 'tree-ness', or form an idea of the 'constant character' unifying all stones, all clouds, a character 'hinted at by all, yet assumed by none'.[82] Further,

Ruskin stresses that a steady and honest beholding of the object is compatible with, and crucial to, any deeper understanding of it in terms of its human relevance, the moral and emotional value of what is seen.

The basis of imagination, he says, is 'a deep heart feeling'.[83] And to Ruskin, there is always for the artist the double duty: to see and to feel. 'The work of his life is to be two-fold only.' True appreciation of fact necessarily involves emotional response to it, and the mission of art is to report this union:

The whole function of the artist in the world is to be a seeing and feeling creature, to be an instrument of such tenderness and sensitiveness, that no shadow, no hue, no line, no instantaneous and evanescent expression of the visible things around him, nor any of the emotions which they are capable of conveying to the spirit which has been given him, shall either be left unrecorded, or fade from the book of record.[84]

A painter who does not recognize the 'essential connection of the power of landscape with human emotion' is merely a 'scientific mechanist'.[85]

Some qualities of scientific mechanism are not, as we have seen, alien to the artist in Ruskin's view. They are important in the respect for fact which they foster. One of the basic principles of education which Ruskin advocates is encouraging a child's interest in natural science; this, he says, should be coupled with instruction in drawing, a skill more important than writing. It is the reverse of education to produce scholars 'disciplined into blindness and palsy of half their faculties'. The exercise of 'eyes and fingers' should come first, as the key to a true evaluation of the world.[86]

He regards his age as one in which the appetite for fact and the sense of fact are both more highly developed than in any previous time. His own youthful history fits in with such an interpretation, while the writing of *Modern Painters* can be seen as his attempt to direct these 'newly awakened powers of attention', both personal and universal, to their proper end. Such tireless garnering of knowledge 'fruitful in accumulation, and exquisite in accuracy'[87] is not sufficient to itself. It is the mistake of some sciences pursuing their deductive analyses to find it so. But rather should it engender those emotional consequences which by their nature will reveal the whole purpose of ardent attention to the minutiae of granite and snow, or to the details of structure in tree and mountain. The devoted study of fact brings with it, Ruskin holds, 'new grounds for reverence' in the human observer. Turner, when he perceives 'the grounds of noble emotion which exist in landscape', is fulfilling the artistic mission in that he sees every fact in its truest character and feels the import of such vision: which is, in a word, the recognition of the universe and all its furniture as 'God's work'.

Ruskin's attitude of treating 'the pure and holy hills' as 'a link between heaven and earth'[88] is central to *Modern Painters*, though it is not one of the more unassailable of his arguments if approached in a spirit of cold logic. There is confusion of cause and effect, passionate assertion doing duty for demonstration, rhetoric sweeping over difficulties. But the weaknesses do not destroy Ruskin's position as he believed it to be, and it is not the validity of his intellectual case which need concern us here so much as the kind of vision he sought to instil in his readers. Beseeching all, and especially the artist, to see and to feel, his aim was to relate the ever closer study of fact to the immediate, instinctive awareness of a divine creator. Nature-lore brings 'such a sense of the presence and power of a Great Spirit as no mere reasoning can either induce or controvert',[89] he claims. 'All great Art is Praise.'[90] Turner is exhorted to make his works 'adoration to the Deity, revelation to mankind'.[91] Throughout *Modern Painters*, Ruskin shows that for him the painter's peculiar fidelity to fact ensures both effects.

This marked emphasis on the pre-eminence of fact in promoting religious emotion helps to place his point of view in relation to the Romantic idea of nature as the language of God. Broadly, Ruskin is following Romantic tradition in taking the view that 'nature could be read like a holy book'.[92] He himself acknowledges Wordsworth's lead, paying tribute in his choice of a passage from *The Excursion* as the epigraph common to all volumes of *Modern Painters*. He might have found many other suitable expressions of the universe's role as divine spokesman in Coleridge, as we have seen. In maintaining a faith in the metaphysical significance of the physical Ruskin joins the Romantic party.

Yet on closer study, it is soon apparent that he has made some important adjustments to the received faith. On the one hand he has relaxed and simplified it; on the other, he has introduced a more exacting approach to it.

First, as in his dealings with the imagination, Ruskin removes the issues from Coleridge's realm of advanced philosophy. The experience of nature was not for him a delight which stimulated his mind to more awareness of itself and hence of a supreme Mind. It was a predominantly emotional experience from first to last. The move to God came not as the consequence of reflexive thought and the contemplation of the world as a structure of intellectual symbolism, but as the simple product of spontaneously associated feelings. 'I never climbed any mountain, alone, without kneeling down, by instinct, on its summit to pray',[93] he says, and he regards 'the mountains of the earth' as 'its natural cathedrals',[94] with awe the emotion proper to their visitors. Although Coleridge would not have demurred, such statements sound naïve when compared with his speculative probing into similar emotional data. Where he begins, Ruskin ends: the emotional state and what it engenders provide proof and answer for him, not the starting-point for research. He worships what he feels to be God's work because of its beauty, while Coleridge, equally reverent, investigates the psychology of worship.

The moral value of nature for both writers is inseparable from their general approach. Self-recognition is the moral as well as the epistemological goal for Coleridge and the symbolism of the visible world aids progress towards that enlightened evaluation. Ruskin remains on the plane of emotionally-led association: the beauty of the physical fact suggests not only the beauty but the goodness of its creator. Henry Ladd says: 'God, truth or abstract idea was not to be seen through any elaborate symbolical representation either in nature or in art; but in so far as they could be experienced at all, were indirectly shown through nature by an emotional inreading of moral metaphor.'[95] Perhaps it is not so much an inreading of metaphor as an over-literal correlation of moral qualities with the natural characteristics and habits of the phenomena he studied so hard. To Ruskin all things in the wonder of their form announced

'God made us' and hence that form yielded moral lessons to the attentive and humble observer.

But if Ruskin reduces the intellectual awareness and the psychological vigilance of Coleridge and Wordsworth to a simpler level of undifferentiated emotional reading, at the same time he promotes awareness of complexities of another kind, not in the subject but in the object. To him the intricacies demanding close study are not those of the reacting mind, but those inherent in stone and cloud and tree. Only by seeing with 'exquisite accuracy' can we arrive at the emotional under-standing of nature, and of nature as our link with a creator; only thus can we learn that from mountain to grass blade, it is 'God's work'.

In this approach Ruskin is at one with the natural theology common to scientists of his youth. Sedgwick maintained in 1832 that science 'deciphers God's universal laws', and William Buckland, Ruskin's teacher, published a treatise in 1837 called 'Geology and Mineralogy exhibiting the Power, Wisdom and Goodness of God'. At this period, Ladd concludes, 'science . . . was performing the romantic function of the earlier poets; it was literally demonstrating heaven in wild flowers'.[96] But the changes implied in this picture of the scientist inheriting the poet's vision need emphasis, pointers as they are to Ruskin's outlook. The science which adopted the revelatory role was one of classifica-tion and close description; its ambition was to read the object in all its detail and the passion for comprehending the character of each thing in itself united with religious emotion. The universe to this view appears not as a vast symbolic utterance whose significance lies in its life within the mind, but as an inexhaustible granary of facts. The centre of interest, in sum, has shifted from subject to object. Ruskin releases the artist from the scientific ends of classification and tabulation, but he argues that unless the most mundane details of the earth as well as its most splendid features are respected by the artist, and fully known in their laws of form and energy of being, the further intimations they offer cannot be received.

Therefore while Ruskin underestimates the psychological complexities of the observing mind, he insists on a proper regard for the complexities of the object. And it would be false to conclude that he is deaf to the Romantic sermon of self-awareness and the importance of personal identity. What has happened in his work is a transference: the personal identity to be grasped is not that of the observer, but of the observed. Not his own inner being compels his 'eager watchfulness', but the selfhood of all he sees around him. His goal, and Turner's too as he argues, is to see not vaguely, approximately, nor according to habits of generalization, but freshly, precisely, and deeply, so that the object is known absolutely as its individual self, performing those functions and obeying those laws of behaviour and form which make it so. Further insights, moral, emotional or spiritual, depend on such a total submission to the object in the eloquence of its self-expression. This is still Romanticism. The urge to savour identity is not ignored, nor has it slackened, but its disciplined effort is now directed outwards, away from the egotistical centre.

Ending *Modern Painters* in 1860, Ruskin says that he has investigated the beauty of the visible world, inviting his readers to share an exercise of concentrated attention on that world, rather than the easier joys they might have expected. He has taught the meaning of seeing, the necessary relation of seeing to feeling, and the need to learn the organization of nature as the way to a true perception of its features: the energies of structure in the mountain, the balancing of the leaf on the twig, the branch on the air. He states firmly:

I have been perpetually hindered in this inquiry into the sources of beauty by fear of wearying the reader with their severities. It was always accuracy I had to ask of him, not sympathy; patience, not zeal; apprehension, not sensation. The thing to be shown him was not a pleasure to be snatched, but a law to be learned.[97]

In *Modern Painters* Ruskin establishes Turner's genius squarely on the grounds of his perfect mastery of the laws of the visible world, and his 'singular veracity': the formidable accuracy of his seeing whether he studies the atmospheric properties of tempests or leaf formation. His feeling for the forces of nature, the destructive powers as well as the 'loveliness and light' of creation is rooted in what he has observed. In his work Ruskin finds the truth of fact to be an indispensable element in the artistic achievement, not a preliminary to it as the *Biographia* maintains, and he lays down his canons of art accordingly. What this means in terms of literary art we may now consider.

(ii) *Objective and Subjective: 'these tiresome and absurd words'*

Sharing Wordsworth's reverence for nature and Shelley's passion for it, Ruskin adds to the Romantic feeling the 'constructive Turnerian element', as he puts it in *Praeterita*.[98] This element tempers alike the Wordsworthian tendency to elevate the pleasure of symbol above that of fact and the Shelleyan merging of the external with the inner world: 'I . . . never in the least confused the heavens with my own poor little Psychidion.'

Such is the gospel of *Modern Painters*, and the section in Volume III concerned with the pathetic fallacy[99] only crystallizes what Ruskin argues throughout. The theory, given its name in 1856, is inherent in the whole defence of Turner, centring as it does on the artistic value of pure fact, faithfully contemplated. But in beginning his explicit formulation of the fallacy theory with an irascible outburst at those 'objectionable words' currently in vogue, subjective and objective, Ruskin shows most clearly that he is opposing, not merely tempering, certain aspects of Romanticism. He is throwing himself across the path of Coleridge's thought and denying the primacy of self-conscious awareness which it advocates. Whereas to De Quincey in 1856 the term 'objective' is taken calmly as a part of normal vocabulary,[100] to Ruskin it and its fellow remain philosophical jargon, sponsored only by 'German dulness and English affectation'. Instead of regarding the currency of such terms as a sign that the relationship between self and non-self has become a central preoccupation and a rewarding field of study for artist and philosopher alike, Ruskin sees in their success evidence merely of human conceit. In his view, they lead to the undesirable conclusions that 'it does not much matter what things are in themselves, but only what they are to us; and that the only real truth of them is their appearance to, or effect upon, us'.

To the champion of Turner's 'singular veracity' such a proposal is heresy. The logic with which he argues his case is dubious but his refusal to subordinate the sense of 'what things are in themselves' to a more relative view emerges with uncompromising clarity. And, putting aside the 'tiresome words', he goes on to assert that the best poetry likewise ignores them, thriving on its detached appreciation of the quality of phenomena as such and not rendered blind by the force of possessive emotion. The difference lies between the 'ordinary, proper and true appearances of things to us; and the extraordinary or false appearances, when we are under the influence of emotion' (xii §4).

Arnold's view.

The greatest poet is not, for Ruskin, one who writes about himself; nor is he one who imposes his feeling upon the object, or makes his poem out of a confusion of the two. He is rather the writer who is strong enough to leave the reader to feel for himself: who says in effect, here are the facts of the thing— 'make what you will of them'. Such an approach is not to be mistaken for absence of feeling. It denotes on the contrary a depth of emotion perfectly controlled, the power to keep the eye 'fixed firmly on the *pure fact*' and to present that factual nature 'whatever and how many soever the associations and passions . . . that crowd around it'. The lesser poet is dominated by his own feelings, and he it is who propagates the pathetic fallacy. He applies to the forms of nature 'terms which should only be used to describe human emotion',[101] calling the primrose 'a star, or a sun, or a fairy's shield, or a forsaken maiden' (xii §8). The greater poet will never impute feeling to the flower or sacrifice it in this way, because for him it will be 'for ever nothing else than itself—a little flower apprehended in the very plain and leafy fact of it'. The art which speaks of 'cruel, crawling foam' because those beholding it are grief-stricken is to Ruskin an art far inferior to that which presents us simply with the 'absolute ocean fact'.

'Acuteness' of feeling is to be balanced by the control of it, and by that coolness of mind which remains able to acknowledge the separate identity of the object, its own nature, even while the emotions exploit it. Dante with fine judgment compares spirits to falling leaves, but he never forgets that '*these* are souls, and *those* are leaves', and such a refusal to imbue the natural object with the human emotion calls forth Ruskin's admiration. He concedes that much poetry moves us because the distinction is not observed, but insists that the highest art, that of Dante and Homer, is marked by a 'calm veracity' which neither distorts the object nor demeans the emotion. Because we are allowed to see truly, we feel the more profoundly. Elsewhere Ruskin says that the function of the imagination is to suggest 'noble grounds for noble emotions';[102] not, that is, to offer us the emotions directly. The imaginative act at its purest stimulates feeling and channels emotion through the object, yet it does so by keeping the eye on the latter, firmly accepted as itself. The emotion is not imputed to the object.

When Ruskin goes further to distinguish between the second rank of poets whose feelings control them and colour their seeing, and a more culpable third category who humanize the object in cold blood, he finds common ground with Wordsworth and Coleridge. To all three, the fanciful personification was anathema, a false trick of style leading only to stilted conceits and meaningless elaboration. But in his censure of all poetry which confers feeling on the object Ruskin stands opposed to his predecessors. He is denying that intensity of metaphor, the fusion of subject and object, which Coleridge and Wordsworth regard as central to imaginative activity. Coleridge transforms the blowing pine trees into 'fleeing' trees as a simple illustration of what poetic vision is. Wordsworth too holds it as poetic truth not fallacy that feeling shall animate the object; to him there is a genuine use of the pathetic fallacy, and he accepts it as 'one of the products of man's highest creative faculty'.[103]

Ruskin's theory of the fallacy, therefore, can be seen as a lever aiding his effort to move the imaginative centre away from the dominant self and towards the object in its independent nature. Whereas the Romantics discovered the rewards of self-exploration and read the universe in terms of such enrichment, Ruskin sees here only the threat of an impoverishing egotism. As F. Townsend observes: 'Ruskin had a strange dread of introspection. He constantly exhorts his readers to look outside themselves. Food for thought must come from without: preoccupation with one's own mind is morbid.'[104] It must indeed seem a strange dread to any post-Romantic mind. Yet it emerges as a dynamic power throughout Ruskin's writing, especially in *Modern Painters*, and it gives him a peculiarly valuable role in the history of the nineteenth-century imagination. On the one hand, he exerts a salutary check upon the over-eager faithful, ready to canonize subjective experience and to debase poetry by assuming it to be merely the indulgence of 'undisciplined squads of emotion'. On the other, since he himself cannot finally evade his Romantic inheritance, he extends rather than destroys the concept of individual identity, renewing it not in the observer but in the object.

The force of his utterances against egotism in art should be seen in this context, as part of a campaign to cleanse the eye, to increase its receptivity, and so to help it discover that the rewards of the exercise are not less but greater than those of self-consciousness. In Chapter vii of Volume III, he sets out his position firmly in preparation for explicit discussion of the fallacy. He denies that there is any place for self-consciousness in an artist whose study is the world around him: 'the whole of his power depends upon his losing sight and feeling of his own existence, and becoming a mere witness and mirror of truth, and a scribe of visions' (§16). Imaginative activity is to be found, not in using the landscape as a means to subjective reverie, but in concentrating the attention so that the object looked at is more intensely seen. Its centrality is never lost as 'all the facts properly connected with it' and associated 'trains of idea' are gathered round it 'in a mingled and perfect harmony'. The power of 'contemplating the thing itself' must exert its control if the 'scribe' is to communicate an authentically imaginative vision, and not merely unburden his emotions at the expense of the 'natural scene'.[105] The alertness, the love and the sensitivity must all be at the service of the scene, amounting to 'the obliteration of the self before the object'.[106] In short, to Ruskin, creativity in literature and painting depends on the 'Seers' not the 'Thinkers'. He charges the simple sensory act of sight with such a wealth of implication that it loses its simplicity and becomes a rare gift, the key to artistic quality. The prophet's title of 'Seer' is inseparable in his mind from the word's literal meaning. Power of insight lies with the one who sees:

the greatest thing a human soul ever does in this world is to *see* something, and tell what it *saw* in a plain way . . . To see clearly is poetry, prophecy, and religion,—all in one.[107]

Reviewing his century's poetry, Ruskin is well aware that his doctrine is out of step. He interprets the decline of an impersonal regard for the world in the light of the modern conviction of God's absence from it. Instead of scrutinizing phenomena with passionate attention based on a 'sense of a divine existence' and a delight in things being themselves as 'God's work', the nineteenth-century artist can only find them significant if they express and reflect himself. Respect for the pure fact is a theological virtue: the inability to face it denotes a man-orientated universe, in which the facts are not only distorted but debased.

Whatever the naïveties of his moral or his literary position, Ruskin's effort to induce the poet to pay the physical universe at least as much honour as the scientist does deserves serious notice. Nature's energies and forms do not exist for human patronage, neither do they depend on our life for the interest they hold: the poet, Ruskin contends, should find his mission in advertising nature's inherent qualities and powers, not in altering them to suit his anthropomorphic instinct. When in practical terms this view leads to the poetry of Scott being preferred to that of the other Romantics and Tennyson, the weaknesses of it are exposed clearly enough. But the kind of point he makes in arriving at this preference does establish a valid contrast which is not defeated by the dubiety of the final judgment. The name of Hopkins could be substituted for that of Scott, and Ruskin's perception of a real distinction of approach in nineteenth-century poetry might then be more readily admitted, since the question of relative value is less obtrusive with this example.

Ruskin says of Scott's work that his 'enjoyment of nature is incomparably greater than that of any other poet . . . All the rest carry their cares to her, and begin maundering in her ears about their own affairs.' Wordsworth, for instance, seems to harbour 'a vague notion that nature would not be able to get on well without Wordsworth; and finds a considerable part of his pleasure in looking at himself as well as at her'.[108] Without conceding that Wordsworth is sinful in this habit, we can accept Ruskin's point that it has its dangers and that there is an alternative attitude which could redress the balance: a Scott (or a

Hopkins), 'instead of making Nature anywise subordinate to himself . . . makes himself subordinate to *her*'.[109] Ruskin recognized that the imagination of his century was prone to create a 'mass of sentimental literature, concerned with the analysis and description of emotion'. In consequence he saw it as incumbent upon himself to declare the more strongly that this was not the inevitable business of imagination, and to promote the cause of 'the literature which merely describes what it saw'.[110]

'Self-examining verse' could lead to poetic myopia, Ruskin feared, and to an inability to ground feeling first and foremost in the vivid sensory apprehension of fact. Negatively, he underestimates Romanticism, and his theory of the pathetic fallacy takes the relating of object to subject on too literal a level, reading it only as a kind of untruthful confusing of the two, wilful or involuntary; hence he belittles the whole concept of metaphor as well as the import of self-research. But positively, the theory seeks to cut poetry free from its psychological bonds. The equating of painter and poet, occurring often in *Modern Painters*, implies that it is the literary artist's function to look out at the world, to be a Seer, with that absolute concentration on the task so manifest in Turner. He is proposing that descriptive writing should be rescued from its comparatively humble Romantic placing in the Tour, the Guidebook, or the journal, and be recognized as creative art. In his own poetic prose, he illustrates his point.

DESCRIPTIVE PROSE

The first volume of *Modern Painters* came 'crying like a trumpet among sleepers', according to a reviewer welcoming the appearance of Volume III in 1856.[111] And many of the sleepers who were roused to enthusiasm by the 'Oxford Graduate' were literary people whose pleasure lay as much, if not more, in the way Ruskin wrote as in his argument. Wordsworth called him a brilliant writer, and Sara Coleridge found his descriptions of nature 'delightful': 'clouds, rocks, earth, water, foliage, he examines and describes in a manner which shows him to be full of knowledge and that fineness of observation which genius produces'. A reviewer claimed that the book was 'the work of a poet as well as of a painter', Tennyson was interested in it, and Charlotte Brontë praised its style for its 'energy and beauty'. The Brownings sum up the nature of the attraction, finding the work 'very vivid, very graphic, full of sensibility', despite some inconsequence in its reasoning and its being 'rather flashy than full in the metaphysics'. These shortcomings are tempered, Elizabeth Browning says, by the thought that it is 'a great thing' for a critic 'to be so much of a poet'.[112]

The critic came to deplore his popularity as a 'word-painter' rather than a thinker, but he was rejecting the misinterpretation of his passages of fine writing, not their presence in his work, nor the proper appreciation of them. The view that they showed him to be a poet, giving new eyes to those who read them, was acceptable because it confirmed his whole argument: that poetic vision lay in the intense perception of 'pure fact', not in the study of self. What incensed him was the assumption that his descriptive passages were merely decorative and could be admired apart from their context.

Certainly, as Lord Clark has pointed out, Ruskin 'set much store by his disciplined observations of clouds, plants, and stones. He said that he bottled skies as carefully as his father bottled sherries.'[113] But his purpose was to show that in words as in paint, nature could and should be depicted in its 'infinite variety, complexity' and 'richness'; that it was the business of artistic genius to stimulate readers 'to see beauties in nature,— in the simplest as well as in the grandest of her phenomena— and to read the laws of her aspects'.[114] When his literary readers recognized this aim and responded to his verbal powers in the light of it, Ruskin had no quarrel with them. Those other readers who found nothing but a series of detachable set-pieces put him in later years out of sympathy with *Modern Painters*, yet he never renounced the gifts and interests which brought it into being, nor the vision it upheld. Better perhaps, he remarked in *Praeterita*, if he had written 'The Stones of Chamouni' instead of *The Stones of Venice*, and so stayed with his 'own proper work'.[115] And in the Epilogue added to the 1888 edition of *Modern Painters*, he writes:

I am glad . . . that the chapters in which I first eagerly and passion-ately said what throughout life I have been trying more earnestly and resolutely to say, should be put within the reach of readers who care to refer to them.[116]

In Ruskin's descriptive prose, then, we have not just a second-class substitute for the poems he abandoned, but his attempt to demonstrate that verbal art can thrive on the virtues of accurate seeing and a sensibility acutely responsive to what is observed. These are the essentials for poetic utterance, he is asserting, this is what the art should be doing, not turning its energies always to 'self-examining verse'.

Opposing Romantic convention though he is, Ruskin is at the same time in sympathy with some aspects of his predecessors' work. Like Dorothy Wordsworth, he is fascinated by the hourly variations in a landscape caused by the changing light and affected by the weather. As she notes the different character of Rydal water or Grasmere at morning or evening, under moonlight or in mist, so Ruskin watches the Alps and the effects of light on them:

On a clear day they change continually: in the morning the dark sides are of a pale silvery grey, exactly the colour of the sky . . . as the sun gets to the meridian they assume a tinge which is not white, nor golden, nor pink, but an inexpressibly rich tawny colour made out of the three . . . They become more golden towards the evening, and . . . just before the sun sets . . . they suddenly, very suddenly, change to the most beautiful pink possible . . . at the instant when the sun touches the horizon they assume a rich purple, which after remaining for a minute or two fades away, and leaves the mountains faint and white and lustreless, yet remaining a long time visible when everything else is lost in the shadow of night.[117]

He captures the sense of the mountains' immediate presence, as Dorothy does with her hills and lakes, suggesting the enduring identity as well as the changing features. And like Coleridge, he responds to the more dramatic exhibitions of transitory effects in nature by attempting to catch them in excited commentary:

The sun is setting on Lake Leman, and I am sitting at my room window watching the opposite outline. The snow on the high point, fresh, is dazzlingly bright . . . I cannot write for looking at it. Brighter yet! Now it is running to the left, glowing on the pastures and pines. Oh, beautiful! The hills are all becoming misty fire, and all is grey beneath them and above. Yet redder . . . it is bursting into conflagration, over purple shades. Now the light has left the bases, but it is far along to the left on the broad field of snow, less and less but redder and redder. Oh, glorious! It is going fast; only the middle peak has it still—fading fast—fading—gone.[118]

The eagerness to secure such fleeting impressions is confirmed in his lament on 11 March 1844 over 'some glorious skies' which made him 'half mad by flying away faster than they came' before he could 'fix one trait of them' on his mind.[119] Coleridge shared desires and frustration of this kind, and in his efforts to fix impressions in his notes we saw that he blended the scientist's alert attention with the painter's sense of colour and visual relationships. Here too is a link with Ruskin, who combined the two approaches from his earliest days, and whose descriptions depend on the resources each gave him.

Ruskin's habits of eye and mind are not without an ancestry therefore. The way was prepared for him in the Romantic readiness to look at and record the natural scene; the immediate literary welcome for *Modern Painters* suggests a public which was not completely at a loss when confronted with such avid scrutiny of cloud and tree. But where the Romantic pleasure in seeing remained an informal activity, material for journal and note-book, Ruskin made it the substance of his art. If we compare Dorothy Wordsworth's account of the Falls at Schaffhausen with Ruskin's, and some of his writing on Mont Blanc with Coleridge's *Hymn before Sunrise in the Vale of Chamouni*, we shall see how Ruskin elevates the observed fact and intensifies the act of observation.

Dorothy's account of the visit to Schaffhausen on 1 August 1820 occurs in the *Journal of a Tour on the Continent*.[120] She writes to convey not merely what they saw but their feelings as travellers encountering a new sight, and hence her description is a narrative with the stress on the experience as it was and is remembered. The keynote is given in the introductory declaration, 'Never shall I forget the first view of the stream of the Rhine from the bank.' The Falls are approached gradually, and we are prepared simultaneously for the sight and its emotional impact. She speaks of the hints of their presence given by 'the sublime tossing of vapour above them' and the 'ever-springing, tossing clouds' which are 'all that the eye beholds of the wonderful commotion'. She goes on:

> But an awful sound ascends from the concealed abyss: and it would almost seem like irreverent intrusion, if a stranger at his first approach to this spot, should not pause and listen before he pushes forward to seek the revealing of the mystery . . . We were gloriously wetted and stunned and deafened by the waters of the Rhine. It is impossible even to *remember* (therefore how should I enable anyone to imagine?) the power of the dashing, and of the sounds—the breezes—the dancing dizzy sensations—and the exquisite beauty of the colours!

Her description of the colours and other features of the cataract follows the lengthy emotional impression, and is comparatively brief. The return to the spectators and their reactions is quickly effected:

> The whole stream falls like liquid emeralds—a solid mass of translucent green hue—or, in some parts, the green appears through a thin covering of snow-like foam. Below, in the ferment and hurly-burly, drifting snow and masses resembling collected snow, mixed with sparkling green billows. We walked upon the platform as dizzy as if we had been on the deck of a ship in a storm.

She remains with the sensations of the day for the climax of the account, the cataract as seen from a boat:

> At first, when seated in that small unresisting vessel, a sensation of helplessness and awe (it was not *fear*) overcame me, but that was soon over. From the centre of the stream the view of the cataract in its majesty of breadth is wonderfully sublime.

Despite the Ruskinian touch of the 'liquid emeralds', it is obvious that Dorothy is less concerned with the exact shades of green in the water and the way it falls than with the range of emotional response drawn from the observers, and the whole occasion as they experienced it. Personal recollection decides the tone and the chosen detail.

Ruskin on the other hand is determined to concentrate the eye on the phenomenon before it. His description of the Falls occurs in Section V of the first volume of *Modern Painters*, 'Of

Truth of Water'.[121] It evinces the 'eager watchfulness' which exhibits nature's intricacy and misses no shade of colouring, no detail of motion or stillness which contributes to the character of a place. He begins not with the expectancy of approach, nor with any emotion at all, but by fixing attention at once on the spectacle rather than the observer. 'Stand for half an hour beside the Fall of Schaffhausen, on the north side where the rapids are long, and watch how . . .': the station is given and the command issued. After this, the eye settles and begins, in Ruskin's sense, to see:

watch how the vault of water first bends, unbroken, in pure polished velocity, over the arching rocks at the brow of the cataract, covering them with a dome of crystal twenty feet thick, so swift that its motion is unseen except when a foam-globe from above darts over it like a falling star; and how the trees are lighted above it under all their leaves, at the instant that it breaks into foam; and how all the hollows of that foam burn with green fire like so much shattering chrysoprase; and how, ever and anon, startling you with its white flash, a jet of spray leaps hissing out of the fall, like a rocket, bursting in the wind and driven away in dust, filling the air with light; and how, through the curdling wreaths of the restless crashing abyss below, the blue of the water, paled by the foam in its body, shows purer than the sky through white rain-cloud; while the shuddering iris stoops in tremulous stillness over all, fading and flushing alternately through the choking spray and shattered sunshine, hiding itself at last among the thick golden leaves which toss to and fro in sympathy with the wild water; their dripping masses lifted at intervals, like sheaves of loaded corn, by some stronger gush from the cataract, and bowed again upon the mossy rocks as its roar dies away; the dew gushing from their thick branches through drooping clusters of emerald herbage, and sparkling in white threads along the dark rocks of the shore, feeding the lichens which chase and chequer them with purple and silver.

This description shows a lavish outlay of visual and verbal energy, with the closest collaboration between the two, and it illustrates well how Ruskin's goal differs from Dorothy Wordsworth's. Her response, what they felt at the scene, engages her most; for Ruskin the feeling is merely the spur to ever more accurate observation, the full reading of nature. He underlines that such is the purpose of his description in his next sentence:

'I believe, when you have stood by this for half an hour, you will have discovered that there is something more in nature than has been given by Ruysdael.' It is not accidental that in bringing out the 'something more' Ruskin's description takes on a Turnerian character. He is attempting to convey the qualities of water's energy and speed, together with those of the light intermingling with it; the relation of the mass of water to the details of spray and dew; and the rich, but water-lit, colourings of the scene. All these elements are germane to Turner's atmospherically sensitive and energy-responsive vision.

Ruskin is not merely the champion of Turner and his inter-preter. He makes the painter's work the standard for his own verbal art, and in so doing, destroys the gap between journal entry and poem which marks Romantic writing. Fact has for him a more honoured place in both the private and the fully-worked published prose. The contrast with Romantic habit is emphasized if we compare his diary notes on Mont Blanc with Coleridge's poetic version of an experience of Chamouni. More accurately, the poem should be described as an experience of mountains combined with Friederika Brun's *Ode to Chamouni*, for Coleridge was inspired to write it in the Lake District and it is partly an expansion of the German poem. He himself never was in Chamouni.[122] But the sentiments of the Hymn, the direction in which it moves, are none the less relevant and are not affected by these qualifications to its credentials as an Alpine work.

A lengthy note preceded the poem at its first publication in 1802, and here the nearest approach is made to what Ruskin would recognize as descriptive writing, with mention of the rushing rivers, the chain of peaks, and 'the beautiful *Gentiana major* . . . with blossoms of the brightest blue' growing near the 'never-melted ice of the glaciers'. Coleridge continues: 'the whole vale, its every light, its every sound, must needs impress every mind not utterly callous with the thought—Who *would* be, who *could* be an Atheist in this valley of wonders!' So far Ruskin would have agreed with him; but where Coleridge then gives full rein to the feelings of a mind not utterly callous in his poem, and concentrates on expressing its visions to the near-exclusion of the physical reality, the Victorian applies his senses ever more industriously to that reality. His energies are spent not in displaying the mind rapt in its ecstasies, but in studying the gentian, the structure of the mountain chain, and the 'whole vale, its every light, its every sound'.

Coleridge amid the mountains writes:

> O dread and silent Mount! I gazed upon thee,
> Till thou, still present to the bodily sense,
> Didst vanish from my thought: entranced in prayer
> I worshipped the Invisible alone.
>
>   Yet, like some sweet beguiling melody,
> So sweet, we know not we are listening to it,
> Thou, the meanwhile, wast blending with my Thought,
> Yea, with my Life and Life's own secret joy:
> Till the dilating Soul, enrapt, transfused,
> Into the mighty vision passing—there
> As in her natural form, swelled vast to Heaven!
>
>   (13–23)

It is a poem of mountain-emotion and of the soul encountering God. The characteristics of the scene by night and day are mentioned—'Ye living flowers', 'Ye Ice-falls'—but only as features immediately leading beyond themselves to 'utter forth God' (69) who is the central subject. The mood is one of adoration and the poet can appropriately say that he gazes at the scene 'with dim eyes suffused with tears' (77).

If Mont Blanc or any scene were to 'utter forth God' to Ruskin, 'dim eyes' were no use—were indeed blasphemy. Not the feelings of the rapt heart, but the accuracy of the seeing eye led him to his intuitions of the divine, and the verbal art went into the visual report. Hence Ruskin's hymn to Mont Blanc may be found in a diary entry such as that for 28 June 1844:

I never was *dazzled* by moonlight till now; but as it rose full from behind the Mont Blanc du Tacul, the Mont Blanc summit just edged with its light, the full moon almost blinded me; it burst forth into the sky like a vast star. For an hour before, it and the aiguilles had appeared as dark grey masses against a sky which seemed as transparent as pure sea, but the aiguilles were edged at their summits with fleeces of clouds, full of intense moonlight, breaking into glorious spray and foam of white fire. A meteor fell over the Dôme as the moon rose. Now it is so intensely bright that I cannot see the

Mont Blanc underneath it; the form is lost in its light. Flakes of luminous cloud hang in the serene over the Pavilion.[123]

When most of this passage is quoted in *Praeterita*, it is tidied a little—the repetition of 'full' in the first and third lines being eliminated, for example, and the expression is tightened, but otherwise it stands as 'a bit of moonlight . . . worth keeping'.[124] This is typical of the destiny of much of Ruskin's informal descriptive writing: it is preserved in only slightly revised form in his published work, sometimes directly quoted as in *Praeterita*, or serving as the substance for a fresh passage as in *Modern Painters*. The diaries were the records of that 'constant watchfulness upon which the statements in *Modern Painters* were afterwards founded'.[125] They are therefore more than raw material; they are themselves samples of Ruskin's art, exemplifying the dictum he sets out in *The Two Paths*:

> good art always consists of two things: First, the observation of fact; secondly, the manifesting of human design and authority in the way that fact is told.[126]

The journal entry following that quoted above—29 June 1844—illustrates how faithfully he keeps before him the need to observe. He feels the previous day's record is incomplete because he forgot 'to note an effect of yesterday evening's sunset' which was new to him. So the hymning of Mont Blanc continues, with further display of his exact eye together with his sensitive colour vocabulary:

> The Mont Blanc was in shade from a cloud, appearing in clear cold white, but on its flanks several fragments of cloud hung in sunshine, pure rose, yet rose darker than the snow. It was remarkable from the centre of colour being not that of light.[127]

Ruskin's chosen art, then, lies in mastering 'the way the fact is told'. In considering this art, which of course involves appreciating what the term 'fact' covers to Ruskin, we can usefully begin by returning to his passion for Turner, and his claim that the painter practises the 'science of aspects'. All that he sees Turner doing with a brush, Ruskin admires as supreme artistic genius; his own ambition, critically, is to reveal this genius, and, creatively, to find its verbal equivalent. Indeed, his championship of Turner may partially arise out of his recognizing the art which lay nearest his own gifts, although in a different medium. He was never merely the disciple, though wholehearted in that role; in Turner he found reflected his own creative mission, that of revealing nature to other eyes. The remarkable affinity between Ruskin's vision and Turner's is pointed out in Cook's biography, where he states that the painter's late water-colours —unknown to Ruskin at the time—have much in common with the Italian diary of the 1840 period: 'many of them are of much the same date as Ruskin's tour; the artist was noting effects with his brush; his interpreter, with the pen'.[128] And each was exploring his medium and developing it, concerned with technical problems in capturing the fact, the writer no less than the painter. Ruskin saw the Apennines from Sestri:

The clouds were rising gradually from the Apennines . . . Fragments of cloud entangled here and there in the ravines, catching the level sunlight like so many tongues of fire; the dark blue outline of the hills clear as crystal against a pale, distant, purity of green sky, the sun touching here and there upon their turfy precipices and the white, square villages along the gulph gleaming like silver to the north-west;—a mass of higher mountains, plunging down into broad valleys dark with olive, their summits at first grey with rain, then deep blue with flying showers—the sun suddenly catching the near woods at their base, already coloured exquisitely by the autumn, with such a burst of robing, penetrating glow as Turner only could even imagine, set off by the grey storm behind.[129]

The challenge for Ruskin here, as in many similar passages of the journals and *Modern Painters*, is one of fixing transitory fact without robbing it of that impermanence which is part of its character. He is particularly drawn to scenes whose forms and colours are dominated by atmospheric features, qualities of light and cloud, merging into the range of watery influences, mist, rain, spray or dew. Mountains in shifting mist, passing showers, spots of sunlight or light fading—all these demand to the full his powers of 'eager watchfulness', and stimulate his efforts at verbal precision. Colours must be distinct, caught to the exact shade, yet the continual blending, diluting, or heightening of tones reported with equal fidelity. Justice must be done to all combinations as they are found in varying climatic conditions—

not only in dramatic Italian sky-clearances, but in the form they take in 'our English mornings' too:

> Often in our English mornings, the rainclouds in the dawn form soft, level fields, which melt imperceptibly into the blue; or, when of less extent, gather into apparent bars, crossing the sheets of broader cloud above; and all these bathed throughout in an unspeakable light of pure rose-colour, and purple, and amber, and blue; not shining, but misty-soft; the barred masses, when seen nearer, composed of clusters or tresses of cloud, like floss silk; looking as if each knot were a little swathe or sheaf of lighted rain.[130]

Colour is named carefully and qualified where necessary with a range of further descriptive words, the aim always being to state the fact exactly: 'dark blue' and 'deep blue', 'a pale, distant purity of green sky'. The 'unspeakable' light is none the less spoken of with every effort to convey its quality: 'not shining, but misty-soft'. Such a textural suggestion is often expanded into the imagery he uses: clouds 'like floss silk', and here the further detail, 'a little swathe or sheaf of lighted rain', in a final emphasis of their nature. The variety in the mixing of light and cloud is caught in discriminating verbs—clouds 'melt imperceptibly into the blue' or they are 'bathed throughout' by the rose light; and the way a scene is imbued with colour is mastered when a burst of sunshine is described as a 'robing, penetrating glow', so that the depth of the light, its warmth, and the way it adorns the autumn woods are all accounted for in a phrase.

The relationship between the ephemera of weather and atmosphere and the solid forms they meet is another facet of this demanding science of aspects, one recognized in Turner's work, as in his study of the Cumberland hills on a spring evening after rain. Ruskin creates the scene verbally with his own methods of stressing the relationships:

> the confused and fantastic mists float up along the hollows of the mountains, white and pure, the resurrection in spirit of the new fallen rain, catching shadows from the precipices and mocking the dark peaks with their own mountain-like but melting forms till the solid mountains seem in motion like those waves of cloud, emerging and vanishing as the weak wind passes by their summits . . .[131]

He is not aping another man's art here, but exercising a different art to tell the facts both have seen. An eloquent phrase such as 'resurrection in spirit' justifies him, as does his verbal grasp of the scene in its elements and as a whole.

The more delicate and vaporous nature's effects, the more precise, not the more vague, must the verbal transcript be. The 'truth' of clouds, or of light and colour can never be exhausted, being new every moment, and vigilance for that reason must never slacken. Words must rise to meet the daily virtuosities of nature. In a cirrus sky at sunset, for example, 'the sky does not remain of the same colour for two inches together':

One cloud has a dark side of cold blue, and a fringe of milky white; another, above it, has a dark side of purple and an edge of red; another, nearer the sun, has an under side of orange and an edge of gold: these you will find mingled with, and passing into the blue of the sky, which in places you will not be able to distinguish from the cool grey of the darker clouds, and which will be itself full of gradation, now pure and deep, now faint and feeble.[132]

From its 'melting and palpitating' colourings to its 'waving curtains of opaque rain swinging . . . from the burdened clouds in black bending fringes', Ruskin reports on the facts of the atmosphere, finding words to keep pace with its evanescent life. The sky descriptions show well that an art devoted to the science of aspects is keyed to the transitory, the moment's impression, and sets itself to demonstrate that in nature there is constantly 'some fresh change' to be studied 'in cloud, or wave, or hill'.[133]

Moving water is as complex in its facts as light and cloud since its character too is one of instability. Ruskin's accounts of river, sea or waterfall show him similarly alert to all variations which they reveal as features integral to their nature. But here he conveys also the suggestion of unchanging pattern and form which water maintains simultaneously with its perpetual dissolution: the constant body of the cataract, the recurring wave crests, the hollows and swirls of a stream in its bed. His descriptions keep the balance of the two, the motion and the form. In the Schaffhausen Fall, for example, 'the vault of water . . . bends, unbroken, in pure polished velocity, over the arching rocks at the brow of the cataract, covering them with a dome of crystal twenty feet thick'. Here, the suggestions of solidity as in 'dome of crystal' are supported by the word 'polished', and then immediately, in 'velocity', are associated with the force of the water, so that both the shaped mass and the unceasing motion are captured, with their intimate relationship brought out. And in examining the range of behaviour in streams as they develop, the 'lines of the water', Ruskin writes:

> the stream when it has gained an impetus, *takes the shape* of its bed, goes down into every hollow, not with a leap, but with a swing, not foaming, nor splashing, but in the bending line of a strong sea-wave, and comes up again on the other side, over rock and ridge, with the ease of a bounding leopard . . . Thus, then . . . we have the most exquisite arrangements of curved lines, perpetually changing from convex to concave, and *vice versa*, following every swell and hollow of the bed with their modulating grace, and all in unison of motion.[134]

The fluid life of the water is not sacrificed to its form, but the latter is fixed on the eye and presented as being equally important to the stream's character. In the characterization of the Rhône, passing 'like one lambent jewel', the same double impression of speed—'not flowing, but flying water'—and permanency of form is conveyed: 'here was one mighty wave that was always itself, and every fluted swirl of it, constant as the wreathing of a shell'. The blue of the sunlit Rhône is another of the river's outstanding features and Ruskin draws on his extensive colour vocabulary to do it justice: 'aquamarine, ultramarine, violet-blue, gentian-blue, peacock blue, river-of-paradise blue, glass of a painted window melted in the sun'.[135] He frequently uses jewels to provide him with the exact colour in bright and active water, as in the Schaffhausen 'green fire' foam, like so much 'shattering chrysoprase'.

Discrimination sufficient to achieve the full and not the approximate fact dictates the choice and expenditure of words, whether the writing is to be elaborate or plain. If Ruskin is copiously adjectival, abundant in his active verbs, or much assisted by simile, he is not in his view overloading his subject, nor using it merely as an excuse for literary display, but simply drawing on all his resources to realize it as it expresses itself. His art is to convince the reader that any lesser treatment would be inadequate, that the cloud or the river or the waves of the sea are objects charged with a complexity which demands acknowledgment by such a taxing standard of seeing and its verbal counterpart. Words can on occasion achieve more than paint, Ruskin suggests, when the complexity depends to an extreme degree on the combination of endless change with intricate formal characteristics which are equally transient yet strongly marked, as in the spectacle of 'breakers on an even shore':

There is in them an irreconcilable mixture of fury and formalism. Their hollow surface is marked by parallel lines, like those of a smooth mill-weir, and graduated by reflected and transmitted lights of the most wonderful intricacy, its curve being at the same time necessarily of mathematical purity and precision; yet at the top of this curve, when it nods over, there is a sudden laxity and giving way, the water swings and jumps along the ridge like a shaken chain, and the motion runs from part to part as it does through a serpent's body. Then the wind is at work on the extreme edge, and instead of letting it fling itself off naturally, it supports it, and drives it back, or scrapes it off, and carries it bodily away; so that the spray at the top is in a continual transition between forms projected by their own weight, and forms blown and carried off with their weight overcome.[136]

The grace and variety of undulating lines in a wave just broken 'might alone serve us for a day's study' (§33), he observes. In this claim lies the challenge to language: the effort to communicate why such scrutiny is called for, and to convince the reader of its rewards. The words must represent the 'day's study' and replace the blurred conventional images of clouds, water, or any features of nature, with their 'truth', their full individuality. A snow-drift is not just an anonymous series of white hillocks:

Its curves are of inconceivable perfection and changefulness; its surface and transparency alike exquisite; its light and shade of inexhaustible variety and inimitable finish, the shadows sharp, pale, and of heavenly colour, the reflected lights intense and multitudinous, and mingled with the sweet occurrences of transmitted light.[137]

No object can be known by its name alone: to say 'stone' or

93

'grass' is no more satisfactory than to use the general terms 'cloud' or 'water'. Identity is only hinted at, even for such apparently simple aspects of nature. Ruskin's seeing and his writing are just as vigorous and detailed when he regards the solid, the less ephemeral, the rooted—however small. He recalls in *Praeterita* how every shoot and leaf engaged his attention:

On fine days, when the grass was dry, I used to lie down on it and draw the blades as they grew, with the ground herbage of buttercup or hawkweed mixed among them, until every square foot of meadow, or mossy bank, became an infinite picture and possession to me, and the grace and adjustment to each other of growing leaves, a subject of more curious interest to me than the composition of any painter's master-piece.[138]

A plant or a flower, that is, is to be 'watched as it grows, in its association with the earth, the air, and the dew'.[139] Ruskin's science of aspects is concerned with the context of each natural object as well as with its personal qualities. He argues that the relation of the grass to the field, the stone to the mountain, the cloud to the sky is a part of the truth of the object. The scientist isolating plant or rock for purposes of dissection is undertaking a different activity, and one which in Ruskin's view misses the vital integration of nature, the interplay of a multiplicity of energies and forms.

The passage quoted above also shows the minuteness of his scrutiny, an exertion which again makes demands on resources of language. The words must capture not only the object in its *locale*, but the details of an individuality distinctly present, even in a grass blade or a pebble. A cluster of grass may be 'ragged and stiff, or tender and flowing; sunburnt and sheep-bitten, or rank and languid; fresh or dry; lustrous or dull'. And a stone

may be round or angular, polished or rough, cracked all over like an ill-glazed teacup, or as united and broad as the breast of Hercules. It may be flaky as a wafer, as powdery as a field puff-ball; it may be knotted like a ship's hawser, or kneaded like hammered iron, or knit like a Damascus sabre, or fused like a glass bottle, or crystallized like hoar frost, or veined like a forest leaf . . .[140]

These studies occur in *The Elements of Drawing*, where the

would-be artist is exhorted to look at the grass and the stone and see what it is really like, out of the myriad possibilities, before he attempts to sketch it. But the work is a manual for the literary artist too, in that Ruskin shows how language can convey subtle visual and tactile discrimination, communicating the full sensuous experience and distinguishing the object, not only as grass or stone, but as this particular cluster of grass and that unique pebble. Similarly 'stone-colour' is dismissed as a lazy and meaningless term:

we have beautiful subdued reds, reaching tones of deep purple, in the porphyries, and of pale rose colour, in the granites; every kind of silvery and leaden grey, passing into purple, in the slates; deep green, and every hue of greenish grey, in the volcanic rocks, and serpentines; rich orange, and golden brown, in the gneiss; black in the lias limestones; and all these, together with pure white, in the marbles.[141]

Turner, Ruskin claims, sees his stones properly and, more than this, has 'perfect imaginative conception of every recess and projection'. He '*feels* the stone as he works over it; every touch, moreover, being full of tender gradation'.[142] Such sensitivity must mark the verbal artist equally and his words must reveal it at work.

As the quoted descriptions of weather, light, and water have already exemplified, words must also reveal the 'exhaustless living energy with which the universe is filled'.[143] 'Tumult, fitfulness, power, and velocity'[144] are all crucial to nature's life, and description fails if it remains static. An obvious point if the subject is a storm or a cataract; but Ruskin carries it further. Turner's painting of water in repose, he points out, contains the memory of its 'past commotion'[145] as well as the unseen currents below the surface, and this Ruskin admires. He is keenly aware of energy as activity, change and development in all facets of nature, including the apparently immobile features. The present condition of stone or a mountain contains within it its past and its future: Ruskin sees rocks, as well as showers of rain or rivers, as their own historians. They sum up in themselves their life in time, the process of becoming, not merely the fact of being. They obey and they express the 'great laws of change'. Engraved in the 'perfect form' of the mountain as it now appears, there is the record of its making by fire or earthquake, 'teeth of glacier' and 'weight of sea-waves'.[146] The clay is recalled in the sapphire which hardens from it, and the soot in the diamond. Sand compresses into stone and marble deepens in colour over centuries of time.

Conveying the truth of fact in nature is therefore a highly testing art, not a dilettante pastime of 'pretty passages'. It calls for a command of language sufficient to communicate, not a single perception, but a multiple vision. To the detailed sensuous report of the phenomenon in its individual being must be added its relation to its context, both in place and time. However ephemeral or however durable, it must be realized in its full potential of energy and form.

At the heart of Ruskin's descriptive writing stands his grasp of these two principles, and further, of their intimate alliance with each other. After studying shells, he notes in his diary for 20 December 1848:

Form . . . may be considered as a function or exponent either of Growth or of Force, inherent or impressed . . . all forms are thus either indicative of lines of energy, or pressure, or motion, variously impressed or resisted, and are therefore exquisitely abstract and precise.[147]

This is his text. Whether he describes the flow of a stream in its bed; the 'flame-like curves' of the upper clouds; the body of a plunging cataract; the breaking of a wave; or the crests and counter-crests of a mountain chain, he sees the 'lines of energy' influencing the whole appearance, and essential to the character he seeks to express. As an artist develops, 'the facts which *become* outward and apparent to him are those which bear upon the growth or make of the thing'.[148] This perception opens the way to the ultimate goal of the seeing eye: divining the inward nature of the object, presenting the thing itself. The master of the science of aspects, the 'great draughtsman', honouring the union of energy and form, achieves the goal:

Your common sketcher or bad painter puts his leaves on the trees as if they were moss tied to sticks; he cannot see the lines of action or growth; he scatters the shapeless clouds over his sky, not perceiving the sweeps of associated curves which the real clouds are following as they fly; and he breaks his mountain side into ragged fragments, wholly unconscious of the lines of force with which the real rocks have risen, or of the lines of couch in which they repose . . . it is the main delight of the great draughtsman, to trace these laws of government . . .[149]

It is the main delight also of the writer dealing in 'pure fact', never conflicting with the aim to display the 'individual character and liberty of the separate leaves, clouds, or rocks'.

The proportion of *Modern Painters* devoted to 'separate leaves' is high, and there is no more detailed study in all the volumes than those on the structure and character of trees. Since the whole idea for the work sprang in a sense from Ruskin's drawing of the aspen in 1842, the stress is appropriate. It exemplifies how much he is attracted by living form, for a tree offers an outstanding example of the 'lines of action' determining formal arrangement, and textural qualities too. As he writes of bark, it is 'no mere excrescence, lifeless and external, it is a skin of especial significance in its indication of the organic form beneath':

it bursts or peels longitudinally, and the rending and bursting of it are influenced in direction and degree by the undergrowth and swelling of the woody fibre, and are not a mere roughness and granulated pattern of the hide.[150]

He devotes pages in Volumes I and V to the 'modes of ramification' in the branches, 'so varied, inventive and graceful', trying to convey all the 'subtle conditions of form' which trees reveal as a feature of their growth. Without losing the immediate sense of its presence as a 'misty depth of intermingled light and leafage',[151] he traces the history of a tree in its visual laws, its proportions, the relationships of branch to twig and bough to trunk, and in the angles of its buds or the hanging of its leaf-sprays. And he obeys absolutely his dictum that the context shall be preserved, the environment shown to be integral to the understanding of the object:

the balance of the bough of a tree is quite as subtle as that of a figure in motion. It is a balance between the elasticity of the bough and the weight of leaves, affected in curvature, literally, by the growth of *every* leaf; and besides this, when it moves, it is partly supported by the resistance of the air . . . so that branches float on the wind more than they yield to it; and in their tossing do not so much bend under a force, as rise on a wave, which penetrates in liquid thread through all their sprays.[152]

Ruskin expends such care over trees and struggles so hard to do them justice, because they fulfil his appetite for 'complexity and quantity' in nature. He is always moved, as Kenneth Clark says in his introduction to *Praeterita*, by 'intricate and rich' effects, declaring himself that he loved 'all sorts of filigree and embroidery, from hoar frost to high clouds'.[153] In the patterning of leaves and waves, flowers in the grass, morning skies, moss on stones, and numerous other instances, he found his passion met. Prepared to delight in the complex, he never reduces nature to simplicity: 'if leaves are intricate, so is moss, so is foam, so is rock cleavage, so are fur and hair, and texture of drapery, and of clouds'.[154]

This assertion helps to sum up all the tendencies of Ruskin's seeing and hence the aims and methods of his descriptive writing. To him the key to a true appreciation of nature's 'variety and mystery' lies in the readiness to allow for complexity on the smallest and the largest scale, and his descriptive prose is conditioned by the need to convey that complexity in full. Words cannot be vague, general and few where the eye reports with a keen particularity. Ruskin's verbal powers must reflect his visual capacity, depicting not merely the surface, but penetrating the object, to announce its identity without loss of force, however tense or fluent with energy, however evanescent, however highly organized it may be. Since he can see that stones are various, or that 'the leaves of the herbage at our feet take all kinds of strange shapes', he must match such variety with the range and precision of his vocabulary. All the words must expose more of the observed facts, and their cumulative effect must drive home the sense of nature's inexhaustible virtuosity. Thus the herbage is

star-shaped, heart-shaped, spear-shaped, arrow-shaped, fretted, fringed, cleft, furrowed, serrated, sinuated; in whorls, in tufts, in spires, in wreaths, endlessly expressive, deceptive, fantastic, never the same from footstalk to blossom.[155]

The abundance of Ruskin's language is perhaps its most striking feature, but it is an abundance controlled by precision, the desire to get the thing right, catching not only nature's 'quantity' but its intricacies. Complexity of appearance is to be demonstrated as part of the laws of being which govern the object, and through the description it is to stand forth in its distinctive individuality.

When Ruskin uses imagery, he does so as a means to this end. Simile is coined, with a relish and sometimes an eccentricity that Coleridge shared, in order to render the particular phenomenon under observation even more precisely itself. He is not responding to the deeper Romantic instinct for unifying experience as Dorothy Wordsworth is when she sees sheep and mist in terms of each other, or the birch tree as 'a Spirit of water'. Ruskin aims only to fix the exact nature of his subject and his use of simile in this way invigorates his prose with a freshness of vision, adding greatly to its force. Stalactites can be 'soft and crumbling like lumps of brown sugar';[156] the moon 'one radiant glacier of frozen gold';[157] clouds appear like 'the scales of a fish',[158] or 'sea-sand ribbed by the tide'.[159] Mountains may be 'twisted like macaroni',[160] or after wet weather, they 'smoke like tired horses',[161] while one day at Chamouni, Mont Blanc 'looks like a heap of earth with four or five good spadefuls of fresh well beaten mortar splashed on the top and beginning to run down; or perhaps, where it is broken, more like a fresh, white, creamy cast of Plaster of Paris'.[162] Examples are unlimited for, as the passages quoted earlier in this section reveal, simile and extended comparison are favourite resources of Ruskin's for achieving vivid accuracy in his report.

The same result can be strikingly won by succinct phrasing also, for example, the 'spectral hackney-coaches and bodiless lamp-posts'[163] of a city fog, or its smoke, 'a rich brick red against golden twilight';[164] at Calais in 1856, 'young leaves lovely, and old spire seen through them'.[165] And Turner's London, by Thames' shore, has its 'stranded barges and glidings of red sail', or 'black barges, patched sails, and every possible condition of fog'. There are 'deep furrowed cabbage-leaves at the greengrocer's' and a 'magnificence of oranges in wheel-barrows'.[166] Ruskin sees boldly and subtly and his language, in its controlled profusion, its concreteness, its richness and its vigour, embodies his vision. He establishes the poetry of description as a verbal art of prestige and authentic imaginative value, showing that to seize the object 'in its very core of reality and meaning'[167] is not an inferior exercise, but one to be respected as a legitimate enterprise, for the poet as for the painter.

Feeling depends on the energy of the seeing. Ruskin reiterates that the emotional response to the object acknowledges its role as part of Creation, and that this perception is only reached by the full absorption of its sensory presence. The business of the artist is to subordinate himself and 'to attain accurate knowledge . . . of the peculiar virtues, duties, and characters of every species of being; down even to the stone', and his pleasure lies in his discovery of the perfect adaptation of everything 'for the doing of that which God has made it do'.[168] Even in all that appears 'most trifling or contemptible', we can find, Ruskin claims, 'fresh evidence of the constant working of the Divine power'.[169] And it is this awareness of a Creator which, conversely, stimulates us to grasp fully the created forms and energies:

> natural phenomena . . . can only be seen with their properly belonging joy, and interpreted up to the measure of proper human intelligence, when they are accepted as the work, and the gift, of a Living Spirit greater than our own.[170]

Intellectually, Ruskin's position here is not profound: we must start from God in order to find him in his works, it seems. And his attempts to uncover direct moral lessons—as in some of his remarks on trees, for instance[171]—can lead to his most naïve and whimsical passages. The fallacy, banished from one door, comes back through another in its most sentimental guises.

His belief in the Divine power as nature's shaping force cannot be held responsible only for the embarrassments of *Modern Painters*: its effects on his prose are more central and more positive. Because he finds that the 'Divine mind is . . . visible in its full energy of operation on every lowly bank and mouldering stone',[172] he is roused to exert all his literary energies in characterizing the bank and the stone, the clouds and the lichens. The vitality which distinguishes his descriptive presentation of the object, so that it lives in the words, is an attempt to convey the sense of that creative imprint with which every living form is stamped and which makes it so intensely itself. Faith in a divine context sharpens his attentive response to all phenomena and sharpens and concentrates his language likewise. But it also determines that his attitude to the facts of nature is simple, the emotional range being dominated by the twin responses of praise and delight. Often in *Modern Painters*, therefore, we find that the effort of seeing completely is followed by a coda of praise and worship in language far less fresh and effective. This ascent to God is characteristic of the work as a whole, as well as giving shape to sections and chapters. As his way of concluding the volumes, he adds a final passage of religious assertion in 1888. Writing 'beneath the cloudless peace of the snows of Chamouni', he reiterates that 'all great Art is Praise', and that

the laws, the life, and the joy of beauty in the material world of God, are as eternal and sacred parts of His creation, as, in the world of spirits, virtue; and in the world of angels, praise.[173]

Ruskin's descriptive art, then, is chiefly marked by its vivid recognition of phenomena, its exploration of the capacity of words to express the impact of identity received from every stone and tree. Energy, form and all sensuous details are captured in their complexity, not killed by language. The individuality of the observed is more important than that of the observer, and the latter is simplified from the Romantic self-experiencing mind to a seeing eye and a worshipping heart.

In his theory Ruskin puts foward the proposition that stating facts is not a prosaic, but a challenging imaginative activity. In his practice he demonstrates that there is a poetry of statement and that a religious vision can be stimulated by its 'singular veracity', feeding on the wonder of the fact as it is, rather than transforming it into a psychological symbol. Although he fights Romanticism fiercely on that front, there remains the irony that the concept of identity, so beloved by his foes, attracts him just as strongly. Ruskin's art is indeed inspired by it. He merely shifts the ground of the research from the psychic to the physical world. The price, in his work, is loss of emotional subtlety and the sophistication of *Frost at Midnight*; the gains, foreshadowed only in Romantic notebooks, are a new grasp of phenomena as such and a new field of opportunity for verbal exploration.

Hopkins was ready for Ruskin's gifts. In his work their poetic possibilities are eagerly taken up and developed, and the ambivalence of their relationship with Romanticism is fruitfully resolved. The place of *Modern Painters* in the history of the nineteenth-century imagination is clarified when we see it between the two poetic worlds of Coleridge and Hopkins, for it provides the route from the one to the other.

3

HOPKINS AND 'THE SWEET ESPECIAL SCENE'

THEORY

'My sonnet means "Purcell's music is none of your d—d subjective rot" (so to speak).'[1] Hopkins offered this robust summary of *Henry Purcell* to Bridges in June 1879 and though it is unlikely Ruskin would have recognized a supporter from the poem itself, he would certainly approve both the attitude and tone of the letter's explanation, for it comes near to his denunciation of 'tiresome and absurd' subjectivism in *Modern Painters* III. Hopkins's reactions to some of Richard Dixon's poems seem to ally them further in a common belief that poetry resorting to the pathetic fallacy, or otherwise devaluing fact, is not of a kind they can wholly admire.

In *Fallen Rain*, Dixon voices the 'complaint' of the rain:

> Why was I drawn through
> All the Rainbow bright,
> Who her smile did light
> Me to woo?

Hopkins is gentle in stating his reservations about the poem, allowing it to be 'the most delicate and touching piece of imagination in the world'. As such it delights him, he says, but goes on to admit that

a perverse over-perspectiveness of mind nudges me that the rain could never be wooed by the rainbow which only comes into being by its falling nor could witness the wooing when made any more than the quicksilver can look from the out side back into the glass.[2]

'However', he adds, 'it is the imagination of the "prescientific" child that you here put on.' He himself is clearly not disposed to write as a 'prescientific' child. He repeats in other letters[3] the same strain of criticism of Dixon's work, realizing that the objections may well shock the Canon, but stressing that he is haunted by the criterion of accurate observation, 'that trouble of perspective'. Images must conform to the facts and show precision if they are to escape his censure and work successfully for him. He finds Browning guilty of 'false perspective' as well as Dixon, and leaves his correspondent in no doubt that, though he acknowledges the charm of a 'delicate personalizing'[4] of phenomena, he regards it as a threat to poetic quality if it entails sacrificing descriptive veracity.

Evidence of this kind links Hopkins with Ruskin as much as the more explicit signs of a connection noted by commentators —'Ruskinese' sketches, the references in letters showing familiarity with *Modern Painters* and other works. If his comments betray irritation with the philosopher, this is balanced by an obvious sympathy with the Ruskin who sees. Hopkins's Journals in particular reveal the affinities between them. The influence of Ruskin is certainly profound and goes far beyond the imitation of a style of drawing or the prompting of alertness in the eye.

But we cannot simply call Hopkins a disciple of Ruskin if the role implies a rejection of the interests and insights of Romanticism. He may dismiss 'subjective rot', but to interpret this as a denial of the Romantic concern with the 'central self' would be fundamentally to misconceive Hopkins's sensibility. The most forthright expression of that sensibility and the intuitions guiding it occur in his theological notes; until they have been taken into account and their implications accepted his relation to Ruskin cannot be assessed.

Meditating on the text 'homo creatus est' while in retreat during the summer of 1880, Hopkins argues for the existence of a Creator from his awareness of himself, both as an example of human nature and in his 'self being', his individuality:

And when I ask where does all this throng and stack of being, so rich, so distinctive, so important, come from/ nothing I see can answer me.[5]

In developing the thought he draws on his poetic resources of sensuous expression to convey above all the vividness of the self-experience as he knows it, 'that taste of myself',

which is more distinctive than the taste of ale or alum, more distinctive than the smell of walnut-leaf or camphor . . . searching nature I taste *self* but at one tankard, that of my own being.[6]

These are not the words of one hostile to introspection or desiring to evade self-consciousness. And since God is the supreme goal to Hopkins, his choice of such awareness as a way to the Creator confirms the positive value which it has for him. But apart from its place in his theology and his Scotist outlook, Hopkins's readiness to savour and explore the sensation of self-being, of '*I* and *me* and *mine*', sets him unequivocally with the poets of his century whom Ruskin admonishes for their egotistical preoccupation.

Was his tongue in his cheek, then, when he wrote to Bridges that his poem attacked 'subjective rot'? To assume so is again to oversimplify his attitude. If he is not merely an anti-Romantic Ruskinian, neither is he just an anti-Ruskinian Romantic. He values subjective awareness, but in his own way. A month before his summary of the Purcell sonnet, he sent Bridges a more extended commentary on the sestet, and here we can find a pointer to his position:

The thought is that as the seabird opening his wings with a whiff of wind in your face means the whirr of motion, but also unaware gives you a whiff of knowledge about his plumage, the marking of which stamps his species, that he does not mean, so Purcell, seemingly intent only on the thought or feeling he is to express or call out, incidentally lets you remark the individualizing marks of his own genius.[7]

For the 'incidental' and 'unaware' display of individuality, the orthodox Romantic would substitute 'deliberate' and 'highly conscious'. Hopkins delights in the revelation of the distinctive self, he cherishes the sensation of it, but he combines this Romanticism with a preference for an unselfconscious spontaneity of being, in which the joy of recognizing the statement of personality belongs to the spectator not the exponent. There is an objectivity at the heart of his approach to self which distinguishes him from his predecessors. He responds to the bird, the man or the artist being themselves with an ardour which testifies to the high value he sets on such self-presentation, but he loves it as it emerges in the act rather than as it beholds itself in the egotistical consciousness. Always alert for the 'whiff of knowledge' of any thing or creature—and the phrase intimates the force and immediacy of impact which he experiences—he casts himself as one who watches for it and is therefore committed to receptive observation rather than more inwardly directed exploration. As we shall see, the role of spectator is repeatedly assumed in his poems: they do not (as he would regard it) lapse into subjective rot, but preserve the stance of a keenly contemplative rather than a dramatic involvement.

Hopkins's notes on Parmenides, made in 1868, reveal how fascinated he was from his early days by the concept, the 'great text' of the philosopher, that 'Being is and Not-being is not'. To Hopkins it was not a concept but an experience: he feels the force of the verb 'to be' in his every encounter with the things of the world, as they press themselves upon him—

indeed I have often felt when I have been in this mood and felt the depth of an instress or how fast the inscape holds a thing that nothing is so pregnant and straightforward to the truth as simple *yes* and *is*.[8]

These notes contain the 'first extant use'[9] of the terms 'instress' and 'inscape'. The context helps to introduce their meaning, and also to show their strength of meaning for the poet. Before considering them, I can illustrate the context further by one of his translations from Parmenides, where the close association of the proposition 'things are' with the sense of particular identity, or self being, is brought out:

Look at it, though absent, yet to the mind's eye as fast present here; for absence cannot break off Being from its hold on Being . . .
. . . and it lies by itself the selfsame thing abiding in the selfsame place: so it abides, steadfast there . . .[10]

Hopkins, then, is moved by a vivid understanding of the verb 'to be', and inseparable from it is his reverence for the often intricate selfhood of all created things from stones to men. Given such a bias towards both thing and self, he was able to develop it by accepting the influence of the Romantics on the one hand and Ruskin on the other. Instead of warring in his mind, the respective champions of subjectivity and the pure fact reach there a new intimacy. He is Romantically attracted to the notion and the experience of personal identity, wishing always to draw attention to it, where Ruskin would only scoff at it. But at the same time he shares Ruskin's ability to allow the object to be prized in its own nature.

In Ruskin's descriptive art, we saw how implicitly he conferred a Romantic vision of the self and individuality upon the objective universe. But his negative view of this characteristic of his predecessors prevented him from either recognizing or exploiting it further. His disciple Hopkins, however, is able to raise descriptive writing to a richer imaginative performance precisely because he collaborates consciously with the Romantic insight. His theory of inscape is latent in Ruskin's powers of seeing, but its formulation marks an advance beyond those powers. For the mind which is capable of coining the term is able to exercise a more complete artistic control over its vision, and hence is able to exploit its materials more thoroughly. Hopkins owes much to Ruskin's verbal presentations of phenomena and to the example set by the sheer energy of his seeing, but it is the younger poet who demonstrates the high potential of such gifts.

All the intensity which the Romantics brought to the study of personal identity, Hopkins inherits, and it goes into his concept of inscape. He needs a term to convey the results of his experience of objects, for this amounts to no less than a revelation of their self being, that 'individual essence' or unique impression of an active identity which goes far beyond a merely accurate itemizing of appearance. To receive the thing in 'its delicate and surprising uniqueness',[11] the full design of itself; that is, to read it and not just see it, is Hopkins's goal. Achieving the goal means arriving at the sense of an inscape and it demands an effort of concentration so great that it is not always possible.[12] It brings understanding, but also love for the object so revealed. In his 1873 Journal, Hopkins gives his reactions on tree-felling, as in *Binsey Poplars*:

The ashtree . . . was lopped first: I heard the sound and looking out and seeing it maimed there came at that moment a great pang and I wished to die and not see the inscapes of the world destroyed any more.[13]

This emotional response is central to Hopkins's perception of inscapes. He is placing the objects in a relationship with himself as observer, an inclusive move which makes his seeing more highly charged than Ruskin's, though the latter's is equally acute. When Hopkins uses the term inscape in his Journals it is a sign that he has reached an intimacy of vision as well as an insight into the unity and patterned logic of the objects at which he looks. The discovery of every inscape is indeed to Hopkins further cause for love, a welcome confirmation that he is not surrounded by a 'disordered field of things',[14] but that 'all the world is full of inscape',

and chance left free to act falls into an order as well as purpose: looking out of my window I caught it in the random clods and broken heaps of snow made by the cast of a broom.[15]

Everywhere, in the behaviour of what is watched, there is identity to be appreciated, the marks of individuality to be divined, the expression of personal being to be discerned.

Ruskin too studied the laws of being and behaviour as clues to the full understanding of phenomena and Hopkins sounds most like him when he remarks on the total experience of a flower, 'the successive sidings of one inscape . . . seen in the behaviour of the flag flower from the shut bud to the full blowing';[16] or when he notes that identity persists through the whole cycle to the end:

It is not that inscape does not govern the behaviour of things in slack and decay as one can see even in the pining of the skin in the old and even in a skeleton.[17]

The self of the object is to be received from the metamorphoses through which it passes, yet the unity of the experience, the sum of the phases, yields its personal quality. Of the flag-flower, he continues:

each term you can distinguish is beautiful in itself and of course if the whole 'behaviour' were gathered up and so stalled it would have a beauty of all the higher degree . . .

Both Hopkins and Ruskin see their subjects vividly in the moment yet historically too; their science of aspects both accepts and transcends the temporal, combining past and future with the present.

We see then how Hopkins draws on the highly developed

Romantic awareness of identity, with its emotional force and sense of relationship, and infuses this into his Ruskinian scrutiny of the object. Moved equally by the 'taste of self' and the conviction that 'things are', he brings the two together in his vision of inscape. He makes possible for himself a flexible art, one which may centre on himself, setting forth his own inscape, or which may express with love the world he observes in its patterns of self being. In both kinds of work he maintains a balance between the intimate and the detached, tempering each with the other, respecting the Romantic creed of inward assimilation and psychological relationship, and the Ruskin virtue of fact preserved as fact.

Instress, the other term he coins, also illustrates his reconciling of the two options. Although more variously, and sometimes more obscurely used than inscape, instress seems to carry two main ideas. One, concerned with the object in itself, and the other, with its relation to the observer. Instress as it operates within the object could be described as the determining energy of that object, the force which makes the thing itself, creating its design or inscape. But further, as W. H. Gardner says: '*instress* is not only the unifying force *in* the object; it connotes also that impulse *from* the "inscape" which acts on the senses and, through them, actualizes the inscape in the mind of the beholder . . . [it] is often the *sensation* of inscape'.[18]

Hopkins therefore maintains within the one idea the autonomy of the object and its conversion into an experience. He sees the pure fact as charged and potent, not passive. It is separate, vital in its independent being, yet because of this very vitality, it as it were solicits the eye which can respond to it. The fact is self-sufficient, but it is only completely fulfilled when it is reborn as a psychological fact. It actively forms one side of a relationship through which it becomes more emphatically itself rather than moving into a more dependent role. 'Hitting the sense' of the observer, it becomes his to love and contemplate only on its terms. Intimacy and detachment, subjective and objective, are again in balance, neither despoiling the other.

There are two other features of Hopkins's theory which point to the nature of his creative work and show how he reinforces his strongly Ruskinian characteristics with a strain of Romanticism that encourages imaginative development in descriptive art. One aspect involves his theology, the other his views on words and poems, and both branch out from the concept of inscape.

'All great Art is Praise', said Ruskin, but in his writing he made only a loose emotional connection between the thing seen and the idea of God, breaking out into a rhetorical coda of generalized prayer after his much more precisely concentrated presentation of the object. Hopkins, however, holds the two together, the created and the creator, in a stronger imaginative tension. He achieves such a unity, first because of the firm theological foundations on which he builds an intellectual as well as an emotional structure and, secondly, because the theology is compatible with his Romantic instinct for prizing the individual and honouring personality.

Central to Hopkins's theology is the Incarnation. He shared the Scotist view that all creation was dependent on it. The world was to be a field for Christ 'in which to exercise his adoration of the Father':[19]

Had there been no sin of angels or men, the coming of Christ would have been the efflorescence or natural consummation of the creative strain; men's minds and wills would have risen spontaneously and harmoniously from creatures to God. But, as a result of sin, natural values went astray and Christ had to perform a violent readjustment of them by his redemptive suffering. The redemptive strain still continues the creative strain . . .[20]

Christ is to be found in the world in two ways, as Hopkins sees it: he is expressed by the 'creative strain', nature simply being itself in harmony with God, and he is mirrored in the 'redemptive', the moral effort and right moral choices made by man which restore that harmony. The poet is conscious of 'the presence of God's design or inscape (that is, Christ) in inanimate nature' and of 'the working out of that design . . . in the minds and wills of men'.[21] He says of created things, 'they are something like him, they make him known, they tell of him', and 'what they can *they always do*'; and of man, that he is created

like the rest . . . to praise, reverence, and serve God; to give him glory. He does so, even by his being, beyond all visible creatures . . . But man can know God, *can mean to give him glory* . . .[22]

In the 'selves' of the universe, and in man's striving to reach his true inscape, therefore, Hopkins finds the personality, the beauty of Christ:

> all the multitudinous degrees of perfection in created things combine like some mathematical formula to express the intrinsic degree of Christ's created perfection. Indeed mathematical or musical terms would be better than logical ones to describe this mystical unity.[23]

Such a vision is, in other words, a stimulus to artistic modes of expression. When Hopkins studies the inscape of the bluebell and asserts, 'I know the beauty of our Lord by it',[24] he is speaking with the full support of his theological mind and also with reference to 'the only person' he is 'in love with'.[25] Hence the statement is so charged with meaning and feeling which he accepts on all levels that it inevitably exerts powerful pressure on him as a poetic challenge. He has a more complex insight to handle than Ruskin and he must extend the descriptive art to do it justice. Yet he must do so without deserting the principles of that art, for the object is still the generative centre. Both he and Ruskin bring the acknowledgment of a creator within the brief of descriptive writing, but Ruskin is unable to weave it and the vision of phenomena into a single fabric. He lacks Hopkins's vital and confident theology, just as he cannot equal Coleridge's metaphysics. And further, with his mind set against the subjective consciousness as an intruder into art, he could not entertain any such unifying force as that given to Hopkins by his welcoming of Christ as a personality to be met in a relationship, by means of the phenomena which 'tell of him':

As we drove home the stars came out thick: I leant back to look at them and my heart opening more than usual praised our Lord to and in whom all that beauty comes home.[26]

It comes home most richly in the poems, where theology is liberated as experience and the art of pure fact is transmuted into the art of the 'sweet especial scene'.

In their approach to the medium of words Ruskin and Hopkins share the view that its business is to re-create the object, to present the qualities of phenomena as they strike the senses, whether as forms single or composite, permanent or transitory. Physical reality is their inspiration and challenge; their goal is to demonstrate that 'things are' and *how* they are. Hopkins, however, is acutely conscious of the close relation between verbal denotation and his sense of a universe in being. More than Ruskin, he establishes his intellectual grounds for valuing verbal statement and its role:

To be and to know or Being and thought are the same. The truth in thought is Being, stress, and each word is one way of acknowledging Being and each sentence by its copula *is* (or its equivalent) the utterance and assertion of it.[27]

Words bring about an incarnation. In seeing their function so, Hopkins upholds Ruskin's faith in their ability to describe, but raises the pressure, so that to realize the thing in the word becomes a kind of selving.

If each word and each ordinary sentence carry such responsibility and demand such respect, it is not surprising that Hopkins has an even more heightened sense of poetic speech. He sees it epitomizing the verbal role and achieving the maximum emphasis, that extreme 'vividness of idea' which is the idea made flesh. In his notes and essays on 'Poetic Diction' (1865) and 'Poetry and Verse' (1873–4),[28] he links poetic speech closely with the structure and character of verse:

An emphasis of structure stronger than the common construction of sentences gives asks for an emphasis of expression stronger than that of common speech or writing, and that for an emphasis of thought stronger than that of common thought.[29]

A poem, that is, is distinguished by the concentrated force of its utterance, the technical demands of verse inducing a special vitality of expression:

metre, rhythm, rhyme, and all the structure which is called verse both necessitate and engender a difference in diction and in thought. The effect of verse is one on expression and on thought, viz. concentration and all which is implied by this. This does not mean terseness nor rejection of what is collateral nor emphasis nor even definiteness ... but mainly ... vividness of idea or ... liveliness.[30]

He makes it clear that he means neither 'terseness nor rejection of what is collateral' but rather the opposite in the later notes where he asserts that the poetic purpose is to stimulate contemplation and bring about the full exhibition of a statement. The meaning lies in the exhaustive presentation of it, rather than in a progression according to narrative or other intellectual logic. The pattern of the one thing in and as its total self is being offered, an experience at once static and dynamic:

> Poetry is in fact speech only employed to carry the inscape of speech for the inscape's sake—and therefore the inscape must be dwelt on. Now if this can be done without repeating it *once* of the inscape will be enough for art and beauty and poetry but then at least the inscape must be understood as so standing by itself that it could be copied and repeated. If not/ repetition, *oftening, over-and-overing, aftering* of the inscape must take place in order to detach it to the mind and in this light poetry is speech which afters and oftens its inscape, couched in a repeating figure and verse is spoken sound having a repeating figure.[31]

Or, as he summarizes elsewhere, 'the structure of poetry is that of continuous parallelism',[32] begetting parallelism in expression and thought. Consequently the poem stands as a 'thing which is'. Not only is it capable of impressing on the mind the inscapes of the world, but in itself it possesses an inherent vitality of design which confers upon it its own distinctive being. It sustains an inscape to be perceived like any other. What it says cannot be separated from what it is.

In his own way therefore Hopkins propounds an organic theory of art and again demonstrates his kinship with Romantic thought. He sees the unity of a work as necessary to its nature and to the aesthetic response: 'the two terms of a parallelism make a whole of beauty, but these wholes again may be the terms of a higher whole . . . I mean only that works of art are composite, having unity and subordination.'[33] Together with the 'energy of contemplation' which is exacted by art, where the mind is 'taken up by, dwells upon, enjoys a single thought', there is also the energy of 'succession', which 'for full enjoyment' is seen as compatible. 'The synthesis of the succession should give, unlock, the contemplative enjoyment of the unity of the whole.'[34] He stresses that such a unity is a complex not a simple state: 'it is rhyme we like, not echo, and not unison but harmony'. 'Difference, variety, contrast'[35] are all included within it, and both the challenge and the reward lie in the proper appreciation of such relationships:

The more intellectual . . . the spell of contemplation the more complex must be the object, the more close and elaborate must be the comparison the mind has to keep making between the whole and the parts, the parts and the whole. For this reference or comparison is what the sense of unity means; mere sense that such a thing is one and not two has no interest or value except accidentally.[36]

Whether in an object or a work of art, Hopkins is ready to discern such coherence as the key to the inscape. In both nature and art he accepts that the further 'the organization is carried out', the greater the effort must be to grasp the 'synthesis of impressions . . . which gives us the unity'.

Ruskin was capable of that effort. He recognized organic unity in nature and the power of his seeing is demonstrated in his perception that energy and form are not merely associated but fused in nature's activities. But though he aims to express this vision of phenomena in his descriptive writing and is ready to exploit words in its service, he does not share Hopkins's conviction that a poem, a special verbal structure, is the means to achieve it. He wins his 'truth' of the object by vocabulary alone, 'detaching it to the mind' without the aid of 'repeating figure', and the concentration it affords. The unity of art, the parallelisms of a poem, are not urgently present to his mind and are certainly not linked to the revelation of inscape, whereas for Hopkins that link is essential.

The descriptive journal note was for Coleridge a preliminary to art; for Ruskin, it was the art. Hopkins, keeping Ruskin's evaluation of the object as the centre of attention, sees the note as at once the substance of art and the preliminary to it, in the sense that it lacks form. A poem, not poetic writing, is the goal. And with his prizing of the creative unit as the supreme means of articulating inscape goes Hopkins's readiness for a closer emotional tie between object and observer. Brought together, they offer him the opportunity for a creative work which is richer in implication and tighter in organization than Ruskin's—an art able to reconcile objective fidelity to the fact with subjective awareness, the reflecting of a personal inscape.

DESCRIPTIVE PROSE

Through his boyhood friend Ernest Hartley Coleridge, Hopkins may have seen Coleridge's Notebooks; he certainly read *Modern Painters*, and however strongly his art is influenced by his theological thinking, he is rooted in the nineteenth-century tradition of factual observation. His Journals reveal this most fully, in their unflagging attempt to record the thing seen with meticulous accuracy. But his contributions to the periodical *Nature* from 1882 to 1884 also help to show his mind and merit attention first. They illustrate that his bent was towards the kind of scientific interest which depends on the most minute study of phenomena, and which necessarily stimulates verbal discrimination and a detailed exactitude.

His letters to *Nature* are all concerned with sunsets: in November 1882 and November 1883 he joins a correspondence on 'beams of shadow meeting in the east at sunset'; in January 1884 he contributes a longer letter to the discussion of 'the remarkable sunsets' resulting from the Krakatoa eruption, refuting observations claimed by other correspondents and providing very specific data to support his own. The three letters are given in an Appendix to the volume of his correspondence with Richard Dixon,[37] but there is another, appearing in October 1884, which seems also to be from Hopkins, and this too offers similar notes, its subject being 'The red light round the sun—the sun blue or green at setting'.[38]

These topics are typical of those filling the correspondence section of *Nature* at the time. The many careful accounts of habitual or peculiar features of weather or other natural events— 'rainbow on spray'; 'iridescent lunar halos'—illustrate how well accustomed Victorian eyes were to such study, and how readily descriptive reports were written. In part, of course, Ruskin was responsible for this tendency but he, and Hopkins after him, belong naturally to a world where both the professional and the amateur in science respect the activity of the sensitive observer; and that observer counts as part of his equipment the literary skill to do justice to the niceties of his visual sense. Coleridge's Notebooks thus anticipate what becomes a long collaboration between a scientific curiosity, an aesthetic appreciation of colours, forms and relationships, and a verbal facility. Hopkins in his letters writes vividly, with turns of phrase or analogy and a choice of words which are characteristic of him, yet what he says stands out from his fellow contributors, not because it is so different in style but because it shows a common approach heightened.

In the Krakatoa letter he catalogues all the changes in the sunset sky of one particular evening, thus offering as research the kind of pleasure he shares with Coleridge in his commentary notes and Ruskin in his long, journal-charted Alpine vigils:

The glowing vapour above [the horizon] was as yet colourless; then this took a beautiful olive or celadon green . . . and delicately fluted; the green belt was broader than the orange, and pressed down on and contracted it. Above the green in turn appeared a red glow, broader and burlier in make; it was softly brindled, and in the ribs or bars the colour was rosier, in the channels where the blue of the sky shone through it was a mallow colour. Above this was a vague lilac.[39]

The touches here of Hopkins's vision and vocabulary— 'burlier' and 'brindled'—serve the purpose to which the whole correspondence is directed, the accurate plotting of remarkable skyscapes. The same striving for exact representation calls forth his resources of imagery, which again are distinctive not for their presence but for their range of reference and a suggestiveness going beyond the ambition of the other correspondents. The 'glow' on 4 December was 'more like inflamed flesh than the lucid reds of ordinary sunsets',[40] he records; and of the 'hollow' and 'swimming' appearance of the sun one evening he notes that it was 'like looking down into a boiling pot or a swinging pail, or into a bowl of quicksilver shaken'.[41] A bright sunset draws out the baroque in his sensibility: 'It gives to a mackerel or dappled cloudrack the appearance of quilted crimson silk, or a ploughed field glazed with crimson ice'.[42]

The letters to *Nature* show Hopkins rising easily to the demands of a scientific publication devoted to the service of fact. In his Journals there is plenty of evidence to support this view of him as a student insatiably curious about his environment. The link with Coleridge is striking and, whether he actually read any of the Notebooks or not, the possibility is appropriate. There is no doubt that many of the entries would speak to him as the work of a kindred mind, an 'inquiring spirit' close to his own.[43] Both move through their everyday world with the liveliest regard for all it offers them, finding themselves assaulted by claims on their attention wherever they turn, whether to sunset skies or domestic detail. Hopkins shares Coleridge's unprejudiced eye for the latter. He is prepared to sketch the 'scum in standing milk',[44] the 'spiculation in a dry blot in a smooth inkstand',[45] or the ice formed on his basin of tadpoles.[46] He notes the 'graceful sprays' of frost on the slate slabs of urinals,[47] frost's 'crystals in mud', and a 'little Stonehenge' of ice pillars supporting clods of earth.[48] There is the same careful study of natural events, 'a little whirlwind' on a pond described in the detail of its motion,[49] water falling in a lock,[50] or another 'whirlwind' of starlings. In the *Journals and Papers*, the editor sets the note on the birds beside one by Coleridge on the same subject. Both are November observations; the circling flocks catch and challenge the eye of Hopkins in 1874 as they did Coleridge's gaze in 1799. Coleridge sees them in 'vast flights':

borne along like smoke, mist—like a body unindued with voluntary Power/—now it shaped itself into a circular area . . . now from complete Orb into an Ellipse—then oblongated into a Balloon with the Car suspended, now a concave Semicircle; still expanding, or contracting, thinning or condensing, now glimmering and shivering, now thickening, deepening, blackening![51]

And Hopkins, as a 'vast multitude making an unspeakable jangle':

They would settle in a row of trees; then, one tree after another, rising at a signal they looked like a cloud of specks of black snuff or powder struck up from a brush or broom or shaken from a wig; then they would sweep round in whirlwinds—you could see the nearer and farther bow of the rings by the size and blackness; many would be in one phase at once, all narrow black flakes hurling round, then in another; then they would fall upon a field, and so on.[52]

The aerobatics of the birds are matched by the agility of the eye in both observers, who are moved to feats of descriptive versatility in striving to convey the fluid patterning, the many merging into the one.

Kinship lies not merely in keen visual response and the desire to record fact. Hopkins like Coleridge shows a speculative turn to his curiosity. He is experimental—even to the point of mesmerizing ducks[53]—and ready for every opportunity to pursue the questions how and why. An entry in his Journal often indicates a whole field of interest, sustained over days or seasons, not just an isolated note. 'The winter was long and hard. I made many observations on freezing',[54] he says in 1870. In the next year, 'clouds and evaporation' are his subject, and in connection with this enquiry he makes one of the most Coleridgean entries in his Journals. Bringing his full curiosity to bear on the behaviour of his cup of hot 'Lenten chocolate', as a contribution to the larger topic, he follows his observations where they lead with that eager kindling of the mind so familiar in the Notebooks:

I have been watching clouds this spring and evaporation, for instance over our Lenten chocolate. It seems as if the heat by *aestus*, throes/ one after another threw films of vapour off as boiling water throws off steam under films of water, that is bubbles. One query then is whether these films contain gas or no. The film seems to be set with tiny bubbles which gives it a grey and grained look . . . [it] is perceived at the edges and makes in fact a collar or ring just within the walls all round the cup; it then draws together in a cowl like a candle-flame but not regularly or without a break: the question is why. Perhaps in perfect stillness it would not but the air breathing it aside entangles it with itself.

After this formidable scrutiny of a steaming drink, he moves out again to the larger issue:

Clouds however solid they may look far off are I think wholly made of film in the sheet or in the tuft. The bright woolpacks that pelt before a gale in a clear sky are in the tuft and you can see the wind unravelling and rending them finer than any sponge till . . . they are morselled to nothing and consumed . . .[55]

Clearly in Hopkins there was a strong intellectual drive to understand the universe and uncover its laws. His appetite for fact is in part a search for evidence from which deductions can be made. Yet in the links he sees between steam curling from a cup and the interaction of clouds and wind, there is an imaginative logic at work based on visual analogy, rather than a more strictly scientific process of thought. This is generally true in his records and points towards the Ruskinian bias of his mind. Where Coleridge sought to press his enquiry as far as possible in his quest for scientific fundamentals and used his observations of the specific object to that end, Hopkins remains much more tied to his immediate experience, his detailed grasp of the particular. His attention is held by the individual object even when he relates one to another: he concentrates his gaze on vapour from a cup or vapour in the sky and the resemblances he finds sharpen his sense of the behaviour and nature of each, rather than lead on to any wider theory of evaporation. His science, in short, is Ruskin's: the science of aspects. In his Journals we find summarized the history of the nineteenth-century regard for fact: the initial Romantic alertness to the world of sense, incorporating a scientific curiosity, maintained by Ruskin but converted also into a keener awareness of the thing itself, the qualities which express its being.

Like Ruskin, Hopkins speaks of the 'behaviour' of objects and the 'laws' which they follow, two ideas which are close for him. To Coleridge the laws of nature were the unifying principles governing disparate phenomena. They were to be sought as keys to a proper understanding, helping the eye to read the universe instead of merely seeing it in its components. When Hopkins notes 'I have now found the law of the oak leaves',[56] he means that he has discovered what gives the oak its distinctive character, distinguishing it from beech or ash. The universe is to be read in terms of its components, by savouring them in their individuality. He dwells on the spectacle of such self-presentation and delights in the display of it: 'A budded lime against the field wall: turn, pose, and counterpoint in the twigs and buds—the *form* speaking.'[57] Everything is to be looked at with the expectancy that it will speak its nature to the receptive eye.

The features of the physical world which recur in his notes from the earliest Journals all show the influence of Ruskin, both in what is seen and the way it is seen. As W. H. Gardner says: 'With the eye of a Ruskin, and the same power of using words as pigments, he glances from heaven to earth, noting the varied forms and changing moods of nature and recording every significant detail.'[58] But it is the degree of concentration on the form, the mood or the detail which marks the real kinship of the two. As Ruskin discovered the aspen in a sudden clarity of vision, so Hopkins is moved to similar fits of ardent perception in which he reaches a heightened apprehension of the object. He describes this state in a letter written when he was nineteen:

I have particular periods of admiration for particular things in Nature; for a certain time I am astonished at the beauty of a tree, shape, effect etc, then when the passion, so to speak, has subsided, it is consigned to my treasury of explored beauty, and acknowledged with admiration and interest ever after, while something new takes its place in my enthusiasm. The present fury is the ash, and perhaps barley and two shapes of growth in leaves and one in tree boughs and also a conformation of fine-weather cloud.[59]

The list is very reminiscent of the 'Ruskinese point of view', a phrase he uses of some of his sketches in the same letter. The 'fury' is the state in which 'the form speaks' to both of them. Whether the medium is drawing or verbal description, the aim is to do justice to that revelation of the object which they experience. John Piper remarks that Hopkins is 'always a *particularizer* in observation' and that his sketches have the same 'explanatory urgency'[60] as Ruskin's. The phrases apply to their verbal work too and suggest well their joint motivation and the quality of their seeing.

Ruskin in August 1880 'studied dew on Sweet William', and saw how the 'divine crimson' was 'lighted by the fire of each minute lens'. He adds in his journal note: 'I never noticed this before—blind bat!'[61] Hopkins would have understood the self-reproach, for he too feels that failure to register the wonders which abound is a serious weakness, although he sometimes imposes 'blindness' on himself as a discipline,[62] this being an eloquent indication of the joy his scrutiny gives him. Sometimes he finds himself incapable of the effort needed to achieve Ruskin's concentration: companions usually distract his eye, and his health could deter him. 'I was in pain and could not look at things much',[63] he notes on one of his holidays, when the sea waves were his 'fury'.

Other entries in the Journal at this holiday time also emphasize how much exertion is involved in the activity of looking at
things, if it is to meet the standards set by Ruskin and endorsed
by Hopkins. Although he could note that the waves to seaward
were 'frosted with light silver surf', he adds that he 'did not
find out much'.[64] And having noticed features of the 'comb'
on the breakers, he must return right to the last moment of his
stay to read them more closely: 'Before going I took a last look
at the breakers, wanting to make out how the comb is morselled
so fine into string and tassel.'[65] On an earlier occasion he writes:
'About all the turns of the scaping from the break and flood-
ing of the wave to its run out again I have not yet satisfied
myself.'[66]

Ruskin's love of filigree and complexity, leading to his
insights into the organization of physical objects and their union
of energy and form, is reflected in Hopkins's Journals. His notes
on clouds and skies, water, leaves, trees and flowers—to take
only his most common subjects—all recognize the challenge of
intricate structure and patterning, whether it be ephemeral or
permanent. Colour, texture, movement and shape in their
various relationships create the object as it floats, grows or
otherwise states its being. Hopkins exercises his eye to trace the
conspiracy of these elements and to chart it in detail. As I have
indicated, his study of waves, especially the shore breakers,
is a sustained investigation and one which illustrates well the
resolution and thoroughness of his approach. It also brings out
his affinities with Ruskin, being a subject equally absorbing
to him. The eye of both is stimulated by the regular and unceasing tidal flow, the strongly marked but ever-dissolving form
of the waves, the light interacting with the water, and the
additional patternings of foam, wind and sand. The sea, in
short, offers them an outstanding opportunity to practise their
science of aspects.

On 1 August 1868, Hopkins depicts a calm Channel sea,

with little walking wavelets edged with fine eyebrow crispings,
and later nothing but a netting or chain-work on the surface, and
even that went, so that the smoothness was marbly and perfect and,
between the just-corded near sides of the waves rising like fishes'
backs and breaking with darker blue the pale blue of the general

field, in the very sleek hollows came out golden crumbs of reflections from the chalk cliffs.[67]

Such delicacy of mood is easily caught, however, compared with the demands made by the character of 'high waves' as seen in the Isle of Man:

The breakers always are parallel to the coast and shape themselves to it except where the curve is sharp however the wind blows. They are rolled out by the shallowing shore just as a piece of putty between the palms whatever its shape runs into a long roll. The slant ruck or crease one sees in them shows the way of the wind. The regularity of the barrels surprised and charmed the eye; the edge behind the comb or crest was as smooth and bright as glass. It may be noticed to be green behind and silver white in front: the silver marks where the air begins, the pure white is foam, the green/ solid water. Then looked at to the right or left they are scrolled over like mouldboards or feathers or jibsails seen by the edge.[68]

Even this minute account does not exhaust the enquiry, since it does not cover the whole cycle of the wave's life. There is still the moment of its breaking and the ensuing behaviour to be 'bottled'. Hopkins admits the difficulty of following these phases but, again, the attempt is made and confirms just how determined is the effort to meet the ideal of total veracity:

The shores are swimming and the eyes have before them a region of milky surf but it is hard for them to unpack the huddling and gnarls of the water and law out the shapes and the sequence of the running: I catch however the looped or forked wisp made by every big pebble the backwater runs over . . . then I saw it run browner, the foam dwindling and twitched into long chains of suds, while the strength of the backdraught shrugged the stones together and clocked them one against another

And in a further note he shows that this effort is not an isolated burst of attention but part of a prolonged programme of visual research, cumulative in its rewards:

Looking from the cliff I saw well that work of dimpled foamlaps— strings of short loops or halfmoons—which I had studied at Freshwater years ago

Therefore it is not surprising that, far from regarding his dossier on waves as complete after these detailed reports, he returns to the subject of breaking waves two years later in Devon, this time advancing to a stage-by-stage analysis of the phenomenon:

The wave breaks in this order—the crest of the barrel 'doubling' (that, a boatman said, is the word in use) is broken into a bush of foam, which, if you search it, is a lace and tangle of jumping sprays; then breaking down these grow to a sort of shaggy quilt tumbling up the beach; thirdly this unfolds into a sheet of clear foam and running forward in leaves and laps the wave reaches its greatest height upon the shore and at the same time its greatest clearness and simplicity; after that, raking on the shingle and so on, it is forked and torn and, as it commonly has a pitch or lurch to one side besides its backdraught, these rents widen: they spread and mix and the water clears and escapes to the sea transparent and keeping in the end nothing of its white except in long dribble bubble-strings which trace its set and flow.[69]

Though he aims at a complete documentation of the waves in their life-cycle, he achieves it without killing his subject, as this last quotation in particular shows. Precisely plotted through the sequence of its behaviour, the sea surges and recedes in his description with its spontaneity undestroyed. Hopkins is master of the patterns of its movement but the immediacy of the sensuous encounter with it remains. His power, like Ruskin's, lies in his ability to keep us in the presence of the thing itself while he demonstrates its properties and exposes the laws of its being.

The same fine balance between the experience of phenomena in the moment and the perception of enduring laws could be traced in his notes on clouds and skies. Like the sea, they are a worthy challenge to the student of aspects, combining the attraction of endless variety with the exhibition to the vigilant eye of well-defined principles of formation and disposition. The early diaries show his meticulous observation, already capable of finding the special qualities even in a 'grey sky at Hampstead': 'Clouds showing beautiful and rare curves like curds, comparable to barrows, arranged of course in parallels.'[70] And in the years of the main Journals he is still alert to the sky of the hour and to what it can teach him in his pursuit of the 'truth of clouds', as in this entry of 1871:

A simple behaviour of the cloudscape I have not realized before.

Before a N.E. wind great bars or rafters of cloud all the morning . . . marching across the sky in regular rank and with equal spaces between. They seem prism-shaped, flat-bottomed and banked up to a ridge: their make is like light tufty snow in coats.[71]

His letters to *Nature* show his appreciation of sunset characteristics, his eye alert for their recurring or exceptional features. Journal descriptions endorse the letters and illustrate how strongly he responded to particular sunsets, eager to stress the individuality of an evening sky with all the force of his vocabulary:

Fine sunset Nov. 3.—Balks of grey cloud searched with long crimsonings running along their hanging folds . . . A few minutes later the brightness over; one great dull rope coiling overhead sidelong from the sunset, its dewlaps and bellyings painted with a maddery campion-colour that seemed to stoop and drop like sopped cake; the further balk great gutterings and ropings, gilded above, jotted with a more bleeding red beneath and then a juicy tawny 'clear' below, which now is glowing orange and the full moon is rising over the house[72]

The effort to particularize the skyscape here, so that its colours and forms are given their full distinction, is typical of his Journals and points to an insatiable appetite for the unique within the habitual. Hopkins's reverence for the diurnal round and the ceaseless rhythm of tides is part of his faith in an ordered universe. But he discerns the laws of natural things because he sees each dawn, each sunset, each wave as entirely fresh, self-fulfilling statements. In the vividness of the moment's experience he understands the recurring pattern, which in its turn illuminates the fall of the new wave or the gathering clouds of another evening.

As the colourings of the last quotation suggest, Hopkins can also remind us of Ruskin because he sees with Turner's boldness and the same susceptibility to atmospheric combinations. All three respond to fortuitous but complex effects of light and colour, using their art to capture such impressions both for the intrinsic pleasure they give and for what they reveal of nature's potential, or on occasion, nature abetted by industrial man, the world of 'rain, steam and speed'. The affinities of Ruskin and

Hopkins can be further illustrated in fact by two extracts from their journals which share the latter vision. In November 1880 Ruskin recorded a sunset observed on a journey into London:

Lasting at least half an hour in full scarlet, only passing from fiery scarlet to ruby scarlet, dark on the green sky, and so into crimson; the whole in majestic depth of tone though so pure, so that the first gas lamps were bright against it while still ruby . . . I must try to paint the way it was crossed by the engine smoke.[73]

Eight years earlier in the Isle of Man, Hopkins too was struck by the dramatic mixture of shades and elements in a 'very beautiful' sunset:

first I think crisscross yellow flosses, then a graceful level shell of streamers spreading from the sundown. The smoke of the steamers rose lagging in very longlimbed zigzacs of flat black vapour, the town was overhung and shadowed by odd minglings of smoke, and the sea at high tide brimming the bay was striped with rose and green like an apple.[74]

In watching the transitory lights and colours in skyscapes or moving waters—sea, river or cataract—Hopkins shares Ruskin's passion for fixing the dissolving moment, and for discerning forms as they are continually broken down and renewed, the dialogues of change and continuity. But, like Ruskin again, he is drawn also to nature's displays of organic form, the rooted life of plants and, especially, trees, where the harmony of energy and structure is epitomized. Studies of trees are numerous in the Journals, his efforts to characterize them as painstaking as Ruskin's scrutiny of leaf and branch in *Elements of Drawing* and *Modern Painters*. Elm, chestnut, oak, cedar, ash and others are subjected to his closest analysis, and the combination in Hopkins of a rigorous determination to read the laws of nature's creations with a spontaneous delight in the beauty of the individual specimens is nowhere better exhibited. The pattern of growth obsesses him, how a tree is organized and made itself, to bring the observing eye such rewards of intricacy and grace. A July note on elm leaves, for example, conveys the analytic sharpness in his study of structure, a sharpness which does not inhibit but strengthens the sensuous contact with the living tree:

they sit crisp, dark, glossy, and saddle-shaped along their twigs, on which at that time an inner frill of soft juicy young leaves had just been run; they chip the sky, and where their waved edge turns downwards they gleam and blaze like an underlip sometimes will when seen against the light.[75]

Similarly in a detailed spring record of budding ashes he shows how his alertness to the visual hallmarks and the formal arrangement of the tree is matched by his awareness of it as a vital and developing entity. First he conducts a thorough survey of the structural features:

The male ashes are very boldly jotted with the heads of the bloom which tuft the outer ends of the branches. The staff of each of these branches is closely knotted with the places where buds are or have been, so that it is something like a finger which has been tied up with string and keeps the marks. They are in knops of a pair, one on each side, and the knops are set alternately, at crosses with the knops above and the knops below, the bud of course is a short smoke-black pointed nail-head or beak pieced of four lids or nippers. Below it, like the hollow below the eye or the piece between the knuckle and the root of the nail, is a half-moon-shaped sill as if once chipped from the wood and this gives the twig its quaining in the outline.[76]

After this exact delineation he breathes the life into the form:

When the bud breaks at first it shews a heap of fruity purplish anthers looking something like unripe elder-berries but these push open into richly-branched tree-pieces coloured buff and brown, shaking out loads of pollen, and drawing the tuft as a whole into peaked quains.

As Ruskin realized that the lines of the aspen fell into place, obeying their own logic, and that he could follow that logic until the tree was newly revealed to him, so Hopkins taught himself to see a tree and its parts as a unit whose coherence is the key to its nature. His notes on the oak are perhaps his most concentrated attempt to reach the full reading of a species as it is offered to him in its individual representatives. He begins marshalling his observations in the quest for the essential oak on 11 July 1866:

Oaks: the organization of this tree is difficult. Speaking generally no doubt the determining planes are concentric, a system of brief contiguous and continuous tangents, whereas those of the cedar would roughly be called horizontals and those of the beech radiating but modified by droop and by a screw-set towards jutting points.[77]

Having established these 'rough' and 'general' distinctions—though they already betray the capacity of his eye—he moves from the diagrammatic to the more specific:

But beyond this since the normal growth of the boughs is radiating and the leaves grow some way in there is of course a system of spoke-wise clubs of green—sleeve-pieces. And since the end shoots curl and carry young and scanty leaf-stars these clubs are tapered, and I have seen also the pieces in profile with chiselled outlines, the blocks thus made detached and lessening towards the end.

The form of the tree is emerging from the tracing of its growing habits and its individuality begins to assert itself in consequence. Hopkins is now sufficiently attuned to what he sees both to single out the dominant features which determine its character and to recognize the licence with which this character can be expressed:

However the star knot is the chief thing: it is whorled, worked round, a little and this is what keeps up the illusion of the tree: the leaves are rounded inwards and figure out ball-knots. Oaks differ much, and much turns on the broadness of the leaf, the narrower giving the crisped and starry and Catherine-wheel forms, the broader the flat-pieced mailed or shard-covered ones, in which it is possible to see composition in dips etc on wider bases than the single knot or cluster. But I shall study them further.

He keeps this resolution, until a week later he satisfies himself that he has fully grasped the singularity of the oak:

I have now found the law of the oak leaves. It is of platter-shaped stars altogether; the leaves lie close like pages, packed, and as if drawn tightly to. But these old packs, which lie at the end of their twigs, throw out now long shoots alternately and slimly leaved, looking like bright keys. All the sprays but markedly these ones shape out and as it were embrace greater circles and the dip and toss of these make the wider and less organic articulations of the tree.[78]

Such exhaustive research into the nature of the object demonstrates how enthusiastically Hopkins assented to Ruskin's science of aspects. His patiently prolonged investigations confirm the contention of *Modern Painters* that physical fact is neither simple nor obvious to the eye. An encounter with the thing itself is won only by intent study, submission to the sensory evidence, and an imaginative sensitivity to the intimate alliance of energy and form. There is a mystery inherent in the physical world as it acts out its processes, self-contained, independent of human will, and both Ruskin and Hopkins seek to acknowledge, rather than to solve, that mystery. Honouring natural objects with the high quality of their attention, they pay a tribute to the unknown universe, discovering its complexities but allowing it to remain itself without being annexed to human systems of interpretation. The early nineteenth-century respect for the notion of identity is carried a stage further as waves, clouds, setting suns and trees are explored solely in terms of themselves, their further spiritual relevance depending on this autonomy, for Hopkins as for Ruskin.

A final quotation from Hopkins's descriptive notes, his account of a bluebell, will bring out both the intensity of his feeling for the object in its own nature, and the way in which its aura of privacy is preserved, not dispelled, by the rigour of his gaze. The personal presence of the flower is achieved without sacrificing its dignity. The science of aspects does not violate its subjects, though it maps every detail of their being:

The bluebells in your hand baffle you with their inscape, made to every sense: if you draw your fingers through them they are lodged and struggle/ with a shock of wet heads; the long stalks rub and click and flatten to a fan on one another . . . making a brittle rub and jostle like the noise of a hurdle strained by leaning against; then there is the faint honey smell and in the mouth the sweet gum when you bite them. But this is easy, it is the eye they baffle. They give one a fancy of panpipes and of some wind instrument with stops—a trombone perhaps. The overhung necks—for growing they are little more than a staff with a simple crook but in water, where they stiffen, they take stronger turns, in the head like sheephooks or, when more waved throughout, like the waves riding through a whip that is being smacked—what with these overhung necks and what with the crisped ruffled bells dropping mostly on one side and the gloss these have at their footstalks they have an air of the knights at chess. Then the knot or 'knoop' of buds some shut, some just gaping, which makes the pencil of the whole spike, should be noticed: the inscape of the flower most finely carried out in the siding of the axes, each striking a greater and greater slant, is finished in these clustered buds, which for the most part are not straightened but rise to the end like a tongue and this and their tapering and a little flattening they have make them look like the heads of snakes[79]

As in so many of his descriptions, Hopkins displays here a degree of visual perceptiveness which seems to make him the perfect pupil for the artistic precepts of accurate seeing laid down by Ruskin in his *Elements of Drawing*. And when Hopkins looks at pictures we find him instinctively applying such criteria himself. Visiting the Royal Academy exhibition of 1874, he notes that one picture shows cypresses 'truthfully slanted'; another achieves 'true drawing of clouds'; while a third, of Goodwin Sands, is 'all clean, atmospheric, truthful, and scapish'. He approves of some 'fine wavedrawing', but is critical of a 'coast scene with wave breaking' because 'the moustache of foam running before the wave or falling back to it seemed a little missed or muddled'.[80] His eye, clearly, is on the detail, and his own sketching—like Ruskin's—works to the same goal of fidelity. It is his limitation as an artist (and an art critic) as well as his success: where Ruskin saw how the hard-won accuracy of a painter could become the foundation of a vision as original as Turner's, Hopkins is more confined to the fact when he sketches or considers pictures.[81] He only makes use of pictorial representation, as John Piper observes: 'rarely do the drawings pretend to be anything but analytical descriptions of things he was at the time looking at closely. He trained himself to look at the objects and phenomena of nature carefully by all possible means, and one of these was drawing.' It would be a mistake, Piper adds, to think of the visual arts as Hopkins's true medium, for 'he thought about painting only in poetic terms', and the life of his imagination dwells in 'the brilliance and freshness' of his verbal art.[82]

The prose of the Journals confirms Piper's view. As Ruskin found, the visual challenge of capturing pure fact becomes verbal also. The word must communicate what the eye has received without loss of sharpness, intricacy or subtlety; phrasing and vocabulary cannot afford to be stereotyped or casual when the observation is far otherwise. How skilfully

Hopkins matched description to his sensuous experience is displayed in every extract I have quoted. In the letters to *Nature*, the precision is achieved by a concentrated economy of verb and noun and an independent sense of analogy, as well as through a vocabulary richly stocked for conveying colour, shading and variations of effect. Similarly in the Journals, but with more scope for exercising these gifts, his writing sustains the individuality of his seeing, as his sketching could not do. Descriptions embody the thing described: the 'huddling and gnarls' of broken waves; the back-draught which 'shrugged the stones together and clocked them one against another', and its legacy of 'long dribble bubble-strings'; the 'great gutterings and ropings' of sunset clouds, their 'crisscross yellow flosses'; leaves which 'chip' the sky, the 'rub and click' of bluebell stalks. Everything which is freshly seen is freshly recorded in language whose impact is physical. It is never over-insistent, the delicate impression being gauged with a success equal to the bold, as in 'little walking wavelets with fine eyebrow crispings', or the observation of 4 May 1866, 'Fields pinned with daisies'.[83]

On the same day he also notes: 'Buds of apple blossom look like nails of blood.' Elsewhere he describes cornfields 'laid by the rain in curls like a lion's mane'.[84] Such images are a favourite resource, again recalling Ruskin. Most of the passages quoted carry examples; throughout the Journals they range from the domestic to the bizarre, with a strong bias towards physical comparisons. He frequently draws on parts of the human body, for instance, to make clear some effect in nature—leaves 'gleam . . . like an underlip . . . when seen against the light', the 'sill' on an ash twig is 'like the hollow below the eye'. Waves fall 'like a shaggy quilt' on the beach, clouds resemble 'sopped cake', and in the Alps in 1868 there is a note very reminiscent of Ruskin, when he observes that the Giessbach Falls resemble 'lades of shining rice',[85] and those at Gelmer, 'milk chasing round blocks of coal'.[86] Ruskin's image of 'plaster of Paris' is found appropriate by Hopkins too, the Rhône glacier in part appearing 'like a box of plaster of Paris or starch or tooth powder, a little moist, tilted up and then struck and jarred so that the powder broke and tumbled in shapes and rifts'.[87] At another stage, the glacier is like 'bright-plucked water swaying in a pail'. The same journey shows the vein of fantasy, as he describes the glacier round the Jungfrau in terms of a tossed 'skin of a white tiger',[88] and the 'edges of broken spray' in a river as resembling 'thousands of little dancing bones'.[89]

Hopkins's prose, therefore, supports Ruskin's in demonstrating that the science of aspects stimulates linguistic energy, and that scrupulous fidelity to fact extends descriptive techniques. In his Journals, however, there is in addition evidence to suggest how Hopkins is to go beyond Ruskin in developing a verbal art on the basis of passionately observed fact. Ruskin's diaries contain the substance of his *Modern Painters* prose, whereas Hopkins in his betrays that he is aware of further possibilities across the boundaries of the prose descriptive account. There is first of all his obvious appetite for words in themselves, an interest which expresses itself in jottings on etymology, dialect, translations, appreciations of individual words, and particularly in lists which associate themselves by meaning, sound, or both. Thus, 'crack, creak, croak, crake, graculous, crackle'; 'grind, gride, gird, grit, groat, grate, greet'; 'flick, fillip, flip, fleck, flake'.[90] Such lists, even more than his speculations on them, reveal that instinct for verbal patterning, involving connection, repetition, and harmonizing, which his theories on poetry also display so centrally. His feeling is imaginative rather than philological, as Alan Ward points out in his note on this characteristic of the Journals: 'Many of the lists could be considered as verbal exercises, sense-variations on a formal theme; some even as miniature poetic compositions in which the meaning or idea common to the individual words forms the subject of the composition, which is given shape by the similarity in form of each word to the other.'[91]

We can see, then, that the Journals join the theory to show that Hopkins's verbal sense is first, highly charged, that he is ready to explore words through their whole aural range and spectrum of implication; and further, that he conceives their interplay to be as potent as their individual force, so that verbal structures take on a special prestige. Poetic organization is a goal for him as it is not for Ruskin, a mode of expression capable of bringing unique power to aid the art of description in its revelation of identity. Parallelism, he says in his theory, is close to the heart of poetry: the full realization of the one thing or idea, 'detached to the mind' by means of its varied reiteration, 'oftening, over-and-overing', with all the devices of verse technique, oblique statement and heightened language. His Journals foreshadow the achievement the theory promises, even in their word-lists, and quite clearly in such an entry as the following, where the contemplation of the night sky yields a harvest of descriptive phrases and images, prefiguring *The Starlight Night*:

> The sky minted into golden sequins.
> Stars like gold tufts.
> — — golden bees.
> — — golden rowels.
> Sky peak'd with tiny flames.
> Stars like tiny-spoked wheels of fire.
> Lantern of night, pierced in eyelets (*or*
> eye-lets which avoids ambiguity).[92]

Accuracy is still the ruling principle, but the assembled possibilities for expressing the skyscape point beyond the resources of prose to an art depending on a cumulative impact, a patterned exploration of the subject where repetition and variety are united in an exposition which transcends statement, however finely phrased. Hopkins hints here that he can lift the prose of pure fact which he has inherited into the elaborate aria of the 'sweet especial scene'.

POEMS

Ruskin, struggling with a Romanticism he was not in sympathy with, broke down as a poet and set up an alternative theory of poetry which could also accommodate his prose descriptive writing. Hopkins the poet profits from that situation, yet at the same time remains in spirit with his Romantic predecessors. Some of his poems stand in direct line of descent from the self-articulating Wordsworth, Coleridge and Keats. *The Wreck of the Deutschland* and the late sonnets alike set out to expose the inner life of emotional conflict and the pressures of a tense relationship. In the long poem, the story told as 'Part the Second' reflects the psychological evolution from crisis to insight which is the burden of Part One: its force is symbolic as well as literal. Here and even more in the 'Terrible sonnets' Hopkins is not only aware of the subjective universe, but chooses to scale the 'mountains of the mind' and to record the kinds of joy and anguish peculiar to his condition. There is none of Ruskin's mistrust for the inner world in this poetry, no reservations about the propriety of concentrating on the 'analysis and description of emotion' in 'self-examining verse'.

But Hopkins is the poet of *Binsey Poplars* too, and here the migration of centre from the subjective consciousness to the world of objects is clear. The 'growing green', its life and death, exercise the poet's attention: the inscape of the trees in their setting is more challenging to him than the feelings they arouse. In this poem, the emotion though strong is simply expressed and the art is expended on what stirs it:

> My aspens dear, whose airy cages quelled,
> Quelled or quenched in leaves the leaping sun,
> All felled, felled, are all felled;
>   Of a fresh and following folded rank
>   Not spared, not one
>   That dandled a sandalled
>   Shadow that swam or sank
> On meadow and river and wind-wandering
>   weed-winding bank.

The pattern and counterpoint of word and line movement provide him with more resources than Ruskin drew upon to convey the living qualities of trees, their relationship with light and moving air, their place in a landscape. The accurate eye is not supplanted. The sensitivity of its reading is on the contrary confirmed and fully brought out by the greater ambition of a vocabulary which is stimulated by the need to meet a structural logic of aural harmonies and visual shape. The devastating 'strokes of havoc' which wreck the inscapes of the natural world are the more acutely appreciated, as are the inscapes themselves, because of an excess of repeated statement which reconciles emphasis with aesthetic control in the baroque mode:

Ten or twelve, only ten or twelve
Strokes of havoc únselve
The sweet especial scene,
Rural scene, a rural scene,
Sweet especial rural scene.

Binsey poplars are selved as well as unselved in the poem,
Hopkins bringing home to us in his whole presentation the force
which those verbs have for him. His theorizing on the theme of
'the taste of self' is rooted in his sense of his own identity
but in its very vividness it promises extension to the equally keen
recognition of all other selves. The example of Ruskin encourages such a development in prose, and finally the perception
of self being everywhere is united with Hopkins's other theories
on the nature of poetic statement, the art of repetition in which
the idea or the object achieves a full incarnation. Only such an
art can in Hopkins's eyes do justice to, in particular, the world
of physical fact, for to him that world is not merely actual but
highly charged in its actuality. Complete in itself, it can and
does attack the senses, asserting its right to be accepted as an
'especial scene' unique in its elements and to be loved for its
individuality. The passion of Hopkins's vision is conveyed by
Binsey Poplars in its heightening of observation by poetic form
and phrasing, as well as in the lament for a lost inscape which is
the poem's immediate purpose.

We derive pleasure from the creatures of the earth, says Ruskin,
because of 'their entire perfection and fitness for the duty they
have to do, and in their entire fulfilment of it'. There is beauty

in the magnificent binding together of the jaws of the ichthyosaurus
for catching and holding, and in the adaptation of the lion for
springing, and of the locust for destroying, and of the lark for
singing, and in every creature for the doing of that which God has
made it do.[93]

Hopkins likewise rejoices in the fidelity of the natural world,
its unfailing performance of its part: 'what they can *they always
do*'.[94] Unconscious self-statement is a condition which moves
both writers and they share the desire to study it in its detail
and in all its manifestations, reading from it something of the
nature of God. 'They are something like him, they make him

known, they tell of him . . . but they do not know that they do',[95]
Hopkins claims, and Ruskin holds that the 'external quality
of bodies . . . whether it occur in a stone, flower, beast or in
man . . . may be shown to be in some sort typical of the Divine
attributes'.[96] It is a short and connected step for both Ruskin
and Hopkins from such relaxed physical fulfilment of mission
to the moral plane, and the harder human role of self-expression.
'Man can know God, *can mean to give him glory*',[97] and is most
himself when he acts in accordance with that destiny, in
Hopkins's view, while Ruskin distinguishes a type of beauty he
calls 'Vital', and defines it as 'the appearance of felicitous
fulfilment of function in living things, more especially of the
joyful and right exertion of perfect life in man'.[98]

In the poem 'As kingfishers catch fire', Hopkins embodies
these ideas, and the two kinds of self-realization, juxtaposed
in his and Ruskin's theory, are wrought into one imaginative
unit, bringing out the inscape of 'selving'. He follows his method
of parallelism, keeping the idea alive before us without seeming
to belabour or overwork the emphasis. First the spectacle of
every creature and each mortal thing in their simple personal
eloquence:

> As kingfishers catch fire, dragonflies draw flame;
>   As tumbled over rim in roundy wells
>   Stones ring; like each tucked string tells, each hung bell's
> Bow swung finds tongue to fling out broad its name;
> Each mortal thing does one thing and the same:
>   Deals out that being indoors each one dwells;
>   Selves—goes itself; *myself* it speaks and spells,
> Crying *What I do is me: for that I came.*

Individual self-utterance is thus 'detached to the mind' in the
controlled 'oftening, over-and-overing' of the lines. It is done
not merely by the art of the repetition which seems to give a
fresh version of the idea each time, but in the additional shape
and force afforded by the movement to a climax of assertion.
This occurs in the final articulation, where the voice speaks and
the poet's consciousness unites with the unconscious self-
exposition. Hopkins is then poised for the next step to the
human version of the idea, the poem thus ascending from the

physical to the moral and spiritual, as is usual in his work. But the method of the sestet corresponds with the octet, the one grows from the other, and hence they are held as one unit of pattern and meaning, meaning through pattern:

> Í say more: the just man justices;
>> Keeps gráce: thát keeps all his goings graces;
> Acts in God's eye what in God's eye he is—
>> Chríst. For Christ plays in ten thousand places,
> Lovely in limbs, and lovely in eyes not his
>> To the Father through the features of men's faces.

Hopkins's awareness of Christ is an aspect of the poem which obviously contributes greatly to its final climax, and the presence in his poetry of this emotion I shall discuss later. But the sonnet, in its organization and the life it gains from the concentrated presentation of its twofold idea, shows well how forcefully Hopkins is able to communicate the vision he and Ruskin share, in the disciplined elaboration of his poetic art.

The point may be further illustrated if some of Ruskin's prose descriptions are compared with Hopkins's treatment of similar impressions in his poems. As reporters in prose they have a great deal in common. We saw earlier that Hopkins's Journals place him with the author of *Modern Painters* in detailed sensitivity of observation and in descriptive ability. His poems show how these gifts are enhanced by his powers of structural exploitation. The desire to respect the object is as ardently felt by Ruskin, and his achievement is not lessened because the younger poet travels beyond him in finding ways of communicating that ardour. Hopkins becomes himself partially because Ruskin first created his world for him and gave him eyes to see it.

'The truth of clouds', for example, is diligently assembled by Ruskin. The clouds are discriminated in their substance and form as well as in their colouring and disposition in the sky. 'How is a cloud outlined?' he asks in *Modern Painters*, using the question to lead into a display of cloud-formations:

What hews it into a heap, or spins it into a web? Cold is usually shapeless, I suppose, extending over large spaces equally, or with gradual diminution. You cannot have, in the open air, angles, and wedges, and coils, and cliffs of cold. Yet the vapour stops suddenly, sharp and steep as a rock, or thrusts itself across the gates of heaven in likeness of a brazen bar; or braids itself in and out, and across and across, like a tissue of tapestry; or falls into ripples like sand; or into waving shreds and tongues, as fire. On what anvils and wheels is the vapour pointed, twisted, hammered, whirled, as the potter's clay? By what hands is the incense of the sea built up into domes of marble?[99]

These questions have answers, which science can supply, Ruskin admits; alternatively, as the rhetorical climax and the allusion to the 'potter's clay' suggest, he would agree that the answer could be God. But his analytical interest does not extend to either. His faculties are absorbed in the fact of cloud shape, the potential of 'vapour' as the eye can learn it. Elsewhere in *Elements of Drawing*, he addresses his powers of characterizing phenomena even more exactingly to the task of capturing clouds in their distinctive qualities:

Now clouds are not as solid as flour-sacks; but, on the other hand, they are neither spongy nor flat. They are definite and very beautiful forms of sculptured mist . . . they are not more *drifted* into form than they are *carved* into form, the warm air around them cutting them into shape by absorbing the visible vapour beyond certain limits; hence their angular and fantastic outlines, as different from a swollen, spherical, or globular formation, on the one hand, as from that of flat films or shapeless mists on the other.[100]

Thus the cloud 'goes itself'. Ruskin's prose is motivated by the need to fix it precisely so that it speaks its individual nature to the observer and is no longer registered as a vague blur, but with sharp sensuous impact. Only on this basis of cloud-understanding can particular skyscapes be freshly received and described. Just such an apprenticeship of painstaking study Hopkins serves—encouraged by his respect for Ruskin's work— as his Journal notes show. But to do full justice to the weather of a specific day, he is ready to adopt organizations of language which Ruskin's prose neither seeks nor desires, though the poet's aim of total realization of the phenomena is, as passionately, the motive of that prose.

What Hopkins sees in a late summer sky is given in three lines of *Hurrahing in Harvest*:

> up above, what wind-walks! what lovely behaviour
> Of silk-sack clouds! has wilder, wilful-wavier
> Meal-drift moulded ever and melted across skies?

And on a more blustery day the sky's character when bright and cleansed after storms is equally vivid from the opening of *That Nature is a Heraclitean Fire*:

> Cloud-puffball, torn tufts, tossed pillows ǀ flaunt forth, then chevy on an air-
> built thoroughfare: heaven roysterers, in gay-gangs ǀ they throng; they glitter in marches.

Ruskin would recognize these clouds. Hopkins too sees that they are never 'flour-sacks', and he conveys in his vocabulary the exact quality of insubstantial buoyancy combined with 'definite form', texture and bulk: 'silk-sack' in the one instance, 'puffball, torn tufts' in the other. The relationship with air movement, whether brisk or gentle, is also precisely caught in the quiet and soft words of the harvest poem—'wind-walks', 'meal-drift', 'melted'—and the more vigorous expression in the other—'tossed pillows', 'flaunt forth', 'chevy' and 'roysterers'. But then Hopkins energizes the whole cloud-vision by the concentration and manipulation of his lines: the force given by the immediate juxtaposing of descriptive terms, the connections provided by the sound correspondences, the balancing and holding of phrase within the flow of forward movement. All the artistry is at the service of the thing seen. It flowers from the poet's high regard for the science of aspects, and it shows how Ruskin's advocacy of that science opened up poetic opportunities for which the earlier nineteenth century was not prepared, in its preoccupation with the subjective implications of identity, rather than the proposition that self speaks from each mortal thing. Hopkins, in the elaboration of his work, magnifies the Victorian discovery.

This point can be further illustrated by the response of the two writers to birds in flight. Ruskin also was stirred by the windhover:

I am very thankful to have seen the windhover. It was approximately at a height of eight hundred feet: but being seen over the cliffs of Gordale, I had a standard of its motion, and when it paused, it was

pause absolute. No bird fixed on a wire could have stood more
moveless in the sky, so far as change of place was considered, but
assuredly both wings and tail were in slight motion all the time. It had
two modes of stopping, one holding the body nearly horizontal, with
rapid quivering of wings, the other holding the body oblique, with
very slight movement of wings and tail. Of course it stands to reason
that the motion of these must be in exact proportion to the force of
the wind, otherwise it would be blown back.[101]

Hopkins, two years later, observes the 'dapple-dawn-drawn
Falcon',

> in his riding
> Of the rolling level underneath him steady air, and striding
> High there, how he rung upon the rein of a wimpling wing
> In his ecstasy! then off, off forth on swing,
> As a skate's heel sweeps smooth on a bow-bend: the hurl
> and gliding
> Rebuffed the big wind.

Both of them appreciate fully the bird's mastery of its element,
the tact and power which it exerts in its engagement with the air.
Ruskin expresses the controlled tension of its hovering, and
combines analysis of its behaviour with the sense of the bird's
presence as he watched it. Hopkins has his standard set for him
in such an account, and his poetic task is to intensify the
experience, not to improve upon the prose witness. Where
Ruskin gives a brilliant report, Hopkins can re-create the bird's
rhythms of poise and flight, imitating its actual physical
manœuvres, the speed and check of its movement. He drama-
tizes the display of strength and grace which the bird offers
and conveys the windhover-quality, its self being, with greater
intimacy and greater sensory impact. Thus the muscular tight-
ness of the 'riding' given in the word order of the first line,
emphasized by the 'rein' image and the insistent sound stress
of the second, is released in the flow of 'off, off forth on swing',
with the free movement of the skating image to reinforce the
change in sound and sense. Then the reversal of tempo, in the
more resistant 'hurl', prepares for the tension of air and bird
again, as the easy 'gliding' is abruptly met by the new line. And
there the balanced alliance of antagonists is enacted in the
phrase, 'rebuffed the big wind'. Hopkins executes his descriptive

lines with an instinct for the freedom won only through fine control which echoes that of the bird itself. The poetry brings the art of 'singular veracity' to a new richness, but it depends absolutely on Ruskin's precept, and the verbal pioneering in *Modern Painters*.

The Windhover, like many of Hopkins's poems, is not exhausted of its interest once the scope of its descriptive powers has been enjoyed. The bird here, the breezy day in the 'Heraclitean' sonnet, are both of more import to the poet. They carry him beyond themselves and the substance of the poems in which they appear is concerned with that development, from the thing seen to the insight generated by it. We are in touch again with the Romantic imagination, in that what Hopkins sees becomes fuel for the fires of his mind, material to be converted into figure and symbol. The bird stimulates his vision of Christ; the transiency of man is suggested by the spoor-obliterating changes of weather. And in other poems too, the nub of their meaning is located at the point where the natural fact meets the human reading of it. *Spelt from Sibyl's Leaves*, for example, plots the onset of evening and its merging into night with fidelity to the event, but the tension of the poem is moral, the theme death and judgment: 'our night whelms, whelms, and will end us'. In *Spring* and *The May Magnificat*, among others, Hopkins registers the season in all its 'juice and joy', and finds it expressing the innocence of Eden and of youth, or his own creativity; while in *God's Grandeur*, *The Sea and the Skylark*, the spontaneity and freshness of nature contrast with the human 'smudge and smell'. In such poems, Hopkins places the pure fact in a dependent relationship, a context which defines its value. His Journal observations, from this angle too, are only the notes for poetry, and stand in the same relation to his poems as the Wordsworths' prose or Coleridge's notebook entries do to their poetic work.

But Romantic though Hopkins is in thus subordinating the physical world to the needs of his moral vision and psychological perception, he none the less remains the descendant of Ruskin as well as Coleridge. His use of nature in the poems at times seems closer to Ruskin's taste for taking lessons for human life from the natural scene than to the Romantic transmuting of object into subjective experience. Where *Spelt from Sibyl's Leaves* integrates scene and state of mind, or the windhover becomes eloquent of Christ's power and beauty, and of spiritual discipline, there is a more formal sense of analogy in, for example, *Spring* and *The Sea and the Skylark*, where the sestet carefully relates the octet's natural beauty to the moral condition of man:

> What is all this juice and all this joy?
>   A strain of the earth's sweet being in the beginning
> In Eden garden.

But Hopkins remains in touch with Ruskin even where he fuses the outer and inner life in the Romantic manner. In none of his poems would the fact yield more than itself were it not so vividly present as itself in the first place. The descriptive detail generates the further vision or application of it. Hopkins's ability to see— the bird, the tree, the cloud—not only survives in his poems to an extent far greater than in Romantic work, it is a central part of his purpose. The first duty of poet and reader is to do the fact justice. Hopkins's notebook is much closer to his poem in this sense than the Romantic journal entry could be. The prose and the argument of *Modern Painters* bring about the change.

In Hopkins's poems therefore we find a double indebtedness, to the earlier poets of his century and to their opponent, who himself learnt from them even as he strove to reject their emphasis on the idea of self and the enigma of identity. Hopkins finds his individuality as a poet in his ability to digest the mixed dealings between Ruskin and Romanticism. His handling of emotion shows this.

To see nature in terms of its 'properly belonging joy' is the business of the artist, Ruskin held. Hopkins bears him out, in that the feeling which suffuses his descriptions is consistently joyous. For Ruskin the emotion could and should emerge as part of the character of the object or the landscape, while the observer who discerns it and through his response reads it as emotion is to be excluded from the art in which he records his vision. In *Modern Painters*, the consequent suppression of the observer as a medium between the scene and its effect on the reader leads on the one hand to a pleasing transparency. There is no intrusive presence between the fact and the recipient. But it is also a limiting feature, because Ruskin has to resort to more stilted methods of communicating nature's joy and its effect on the heart. While he allows the sheer power of his description to make its own impression, the feeling can seem to take care of itself. In displaying the delicacy, the virtuosity, the 'buoyancy and elasticity of inward energy'[102] which mark the forms of nature, he conveys a zest and a vitality, which can be interpreted as spontaneous gladness of being. Such feeling and the full statement of the phenomena are then inseparable. But Ruskin also seeks to render the emotion explicitly and his attempts to circumvent the menace of subjective emphasis are of doubtful success. He has recourse, for example, to rhetorical exclamation and the somewhat playful use of personification. Describing the pleasant combination of rain and streams in temperate climates, he refers to the 'soft wings of the Sea Angel', the rainclouds which float over the hills where 'strange laughings and glitterings of silver streamlets, born suddenly, and twined about the mossy heights in trickling tinsel' answer to them 'as they wave'.[103] And the joy of high mountains becomes a presentation of 'fiery peaks, which, with heaving bosoms and exulting limbs, with the clouds drifting like hair from their bright foreheads, lift up their Titan hands to heaven, saying, "I live for ever!"'[104]

Hopkins is not troubled by the fear that to admit the subjective response is to muddy the waters of pure fact. As part of his poetic structure he adopts the text given in *Hurrahing in Harvest*: 'These things, these things were here and but the beholder Wanting', and the question asked in *Ribblesdale*:

> And what is Earth's eye, tongue, or heart else, where
> Else, but in dear and dogged man?

For him the conjunction of observed with observer—'which two when they once meet'—is the creative moment, leading not to the diminishing of the fact but to its greater accessibility. Because the harvest landscape or the windhover are acknowledged as events in the mind, generating emotion in the heart which is stirred by them, Hopkins is able to integrate fact and feeling. There is no need to smuggle the latter into his poem, nor to resort to devious whimsicalities. He himself is in the poem—

but in the role of observer, reacting to what he sees: the descriptive care is not lessened by the poet's presence. Rather the faithful report of what is seen justifies his emotional comment on it. The balance therefore is changed from the Romantic apportioning of fact and reaction, where the latter was paramount. Hopkins gives himself the opportunity for a movement inward, and is ready enough to accept it, but the progression to symbol is not inevitable, the thing seen is allowed to remain itself, and the experience of the poem is that of feeling roused by impassioned observation. Emotion acts as a spotlight illuminating the object, while at the same time its presence as the personal response, a tone of voice, engages the reader more intimately, making him aware of that observing consciousness as a further quality in the poem. Hopkins's directives: 'Look at the stars!'; his questions and admonitions— 'have, get, before it cloy'; his simple statements and exclamations: 'my heart in hiding Stirred for a bird,—the achieve of, the mastery of the thing!'; all these extend his poetic range and never work to obscure the sensuous encounter with what is seen. His vision of sunrise at the end of *God's Grandeur* gives a striking instance of an emotional pointer being timed so that it adds a final calculated emphasis:

> Oh, morning, at the brown brink eastward, springs—
> Because the Holy Ghost over the bent
> World broods with warm breast and with ah! bright wings.

'Oh' and 'ah' on the face of it are words for a lazy poet but here they are functional. The coming of light is suggested the more accurately in its sudden glory because it is introduced by the spectator's exclamation which provides the keynote of excitement and wonder. The word order is managed so that this mood is sustained, and the check to the movement provided by the 'ah!' not only heightens the feeling to a climax but punctuates the line, arresting it just sufficiently for the 'bright' which follows it to burst upon the mind with the force of revelation. Hopkins shows here how he fuses all resources of structure, vocabulary and rhythm with those of explicit feeling to renew the facts of nature.

The lines from *God's Grandeur* also raise one final point about his ability to make his poetic voice out of Romanticism and Ruskin brought together. The bold identification of the sun with the Holy Ghost as dove is only one of the solutions Hopkins finds to bring about the integration, not merely of feeling with fact, but of his religious awareness with the thing seen. Again, he has more resources than Ruskin because he is able to exploit symbol and to incorporate himself and his personal relationships into his presentation of the physical scene. Where Ruskin felt obliged to exclude the intimate responses of the subjective consciousness, Hopkins can welcome them as a means of expressing the conviction he shares with Ruskin, that 'the knowledge of what is beautiful leads on', and 'all great Art is Praise'.[105]

Nature properly seen, Ruskin believed, gives insight into the 'living Spirit' of a Creator. But his efforts in *Modern Painters* to show this faith, either as an argument or an experience, tend to be unconvincing, being intellectually confused and emotionally crude. There is always a gap between the finely realized object and the much weaker conventional formulae in which he seeks to convey its religious import. Invocation and the more pompous gestures of worship, conceived as the climax to a descriptive passage into which all his energies have been gathered, stand only as anticlimax. Thus after detailed sketches by which he invites his reader to watch with him some of the 'skies of nature' attempted by painters—the dawn 'flakes of light', the 'green halo' of a rising moon—he reaches the significance of his descriptions:

and then, when you can look no more for gladness, and when you are bowed down with fear and love of the Maker and Doer of this, tell me who has best delivered His message unto men![106]

Neither God nor Turner is vividly discovered in such a conclusion, and though the latter is much more concretely present in the five volumes wherever Ruskin is exercising his gift for vital description, God is not so well served, remaining throughout a pious concept, addressed in a special voice which lacks the convincing ring of the Ruskin closely engaged with descriptive report. The general inhibiting of emotional freedom affects the religious vision together with the communication of that personal joy which relates to it. God may be acknowledged as the Maker and Doer, but he is not directly felt in relation to what he has made and done, nor to the speaker who observes creation and then addresses its creator. Ruskin's crusade against the engulfing tides of subjectivity and self-articulation forbids the development of any more immediate sense of a triangular relationship, wherein the observer's emotion could bind all together and provide the medium through which the presence of an intimate bond between God and his 'work' could be experienced.

Hopkins, on the other hand, does not resist the Romantic instinct to relate the world of sense to the whole personality, and he reads his life in terms of relationships. He sees himself modified by other things or persons, and in his turn modifying them. Understanding comes to him through the experience of selves meeting, his own with the other, and both are revealed to him by this means. As his relationship with God is central to him, it is inevitable that his encounters with the physical world he also loves shall have some bearing on that relationship; the connection is not only possible for him but inescapable. In his poems he is able to show how his feelings of love for and joy in nature flower spontaneously into a vivid apprehension of God. He presents himself and his feelings as the pivot by which the transition from natural to supernatural can be easily made with no loss of impact.

> I walk, I lift up, I lift up heart, eyes,
> Down all that glory in the heavens to glean our Saviour;
> And eýes, héart, what looks, what lips yet gave you a
> Rapturous love's greeting of realer, of rounder replies?

Out of the intimacy of the lover recognizing his beloved comes the *Hurrahing in Harvest* vision of the 'azurous hung hills' as his 'world-wielding shoulder', a coalescence in which both the hills and Christ are honoured without loss of identity, yet each is rendered an experience to the observer beyond that of isolated pure fact or conventional religious sentiment. Hopkins is helped of course in his handling of the relation between divine and natural by his theology of the Incarnation, his perception of Christ as a person loving and to be loved and also as present in the created universe, epitomizing its role of adoration through the simple fulfilment of its being. The 'Maker' and 'Doer' can be called upon as Christ or approached through Christ, and in both instances, he ceases to be an aloof and formal deity. The ascent to God is characteristic of the movement in his poems, but it is an integrated progression, prompted by the full acceptance of phenomena as themselves, together with his own emotional states of joy and love. *The Windhover* dedicated to 'Christ our Lord', shows how the sensuous revelation is for Hopkins immediately the channel for the spiritual, the greater recognition of both the God he loves and his own moral identity. Catching the way a bird flies and is itself, he is moved to see how Christ is, and how he himself must labour and love to become so poised a being.

In Hopkins's poetry, therefore, the science of aspects becomes a more complex art and embraces a wider range of implication than it does in Ruskin's pursuit of it. Yet without Ruskin, Hopkins's sense of the 'sweet especial scene' might well have remained undeveloped in itself and as a feature of his poems. In his work we can see more clearly how Ruskin's apparent rejection of the strongest tendencies of the contemporary imagination was in fact neither an entire repudiation nor a merely negative resistance. By fighting for the dignity of the object, distinct and apart from human designs upon it, Ruskin transferred the Romantic respect for the mystery of identity to a different centre, rather than denied it as an inspiration. He made possible, because he too saw, what Hopkins delights in: that each thing 'selves—goes itself'. This extension of vision was liberating, a protection from the extreme consequences of Romantic self-absorption, against which Ruskin warns in his arguments under the heading of 'pathetic fallacy'. Such a redressing of balance was beneficial, opening up as it did this other science and art of aspects, promoting it from the secondary role of notebook material—in which place, as Coleridge eloquently shows, it was already a feature of Romantic awareness—to poetic status. *Modern Painters* is no aberration in the history of the nineteenth-century imagination but a contribution of profound importance to its development from early Romanticism. Hopkins presents the revised version of Romanticism possible to one who inherited *Modern Painters* yet at the same time remained branded by the earlier poets. Polemic against them was necessary to Ruskin, but its outcome for his descendants is to renew rather than to sever contact. Subjective and objective withstand abuse as 'tiresome and absurd' and survive in a relationship vital for creative art, but with a new balance and reciprocity for a poet of Hopkins's powers to reveal. He takes for his text the extended awareness that of all things, not just the human consciousness, it is true that 'self flashes off frame and face'.

Romantics were primarily subjective;
Ruskin was " objective;
Hopkins balanced the two.

APPENDIX

AN UNCOLLECTED LETTER FROM HOPKINS TO *NATURE*, 30 OCTOBER 1884

The Red Light round the Sun—The Sun Blue or Green at Setting

I can confirm Mr. Backhouse's and Mr. E. D. Archibald's impression about the colour now and for some time past seen round the sun; that it first appeared about November last and has been more or less visible ever since. The colour was then, and still is, sometimes rose, sometimes amber or buff. It is best observed, when the sun on bright days is behind a cloud, round that cloud, in the place where, at other times, broken beams of shadow, thrown out from the cloud like a row of irregular palings and deepening the blue of the sky, are to be seen. Towards sunset it becomes glaring, and white and sallow in hue. Something of a circular shape may then perhaps be made out in it, but it does not seem to me that it ought to be called a halo. A halo, as I understand, is a ring, or at least a round space inclosed by a ring. This appearance has no ring round it. Also in a halo (I have seen numbers) it is the ring that is coloured— either throughout, or at four places where the ends of the four arms of a cross would rest upon it; and the inclosed field is uncoloured or coloured like the rest of the sky: here there is an uninclosed but singularly-coloured field.

But whether we call the appearance a halo or not is perhaps only a question of terms: to call it a corona, as Mr. Leslie does, is another, and, as it seems to me, a hazardous thing, because it would imply that what we are looking at is an appendage of the sun's own (and that too at a time when it is strongly doubted if the sun has a corona of any sort of all), instead of what is much easier to suppose, a terrestrial or atmospheric effect. If there is going on, as Mr. Leslie thinks, an 'increase of sun power', this ought to be both felt and measured by exact instruments, not by the untrustworthy impressions of the eye. Now Prof.

Piazzi-Smyth says that sunlight, as tested by the spectroscope, is weaker, not stronger, since the phenomena of last winter began. To set down variations in light and heat to changes in the sun when they may be explained by changes in our atmosphere, is like preferring the Ptolemaic to the Copernican system.

It is, however, right and important to distinguish phenomena really new from old ones first observed under new circumstances which make people unusually observant. A sun seen as green or blue for hours together is a phenomenon only witnessed after the late Krakatoa eruptions (barring some rare reports of like appearances after like outbreaks, and under other exceptional conditions); but a sun which turns green or blue just at setting is, I believe, an old and, we may say, ordinary one, little remarked till lately. I have a note of witnessing it, with other persons of a company, in North Wales on June 23, 1877, the sunset being very clear and bright. It is, possibly, an optical effect only, due to a reaction (from the red or yellow sunset light, to its complementary colour) taking place in the over-strained eye at the moment when the light is suddenly cut off, either by the sun's disappearance or by his entering a much thicker belt of vapour, which, foreshortened as the vapour is close to the horizon, may happen almost instantaneously. And this is confirmed by a kindred phenomenon of sunset. If a very clear, unclouded sun is then gazed at, it often appears not convex, but hollow; swimming—like looking down into a boiling pot or a swinging pail, or into a bowl of quicksilver shaken; and of a lustrous but indistinct blue. The sky about it appears to swell up all round into a lip or brim, and this brim is coloured pink. The colour of the light will at that time be (though the eye becomes deadened to it) between red and yellow. Now it may be noticed that when a candle-flame is looked at through coloured glass, though everything else behind the glass is strongly stained with the colour, the flame is often nearly white: I suppose the light direct from the sun's disk not only to master the red and yellow of the vapour medium, but even, to the eye, to take on something of the complementary blue.

Even since writing the above I have witnessed, though slightly, the phenomenon of a blue setting. The sunset was bright this evening, the sun of a ruddy gold, which colour it kept till nothing was left of it but a star-like spot; then this spot turned, for the twinkling of an eye, a leaden or watery blue, and vanished.

There followed a glow as bright almost as those of last year. Between 6.15 and 6.30 (Dublin time) it was intense: bronzy near the earth; above like peach, or of the blush colour on ripe hazels. It drew away southwards. It would seem as if the volcanic 'wrack' had become a satellite to the earth, like Saturn's rings, and was subject to phases, of which we are now witnessing a vivid one.

Dublin, October 19   G.M.H.

BIBLIOGRAPHY

I. EDITIONS OF POETRY AND PROSE

Biographia Literaria and Aesthetical Essays, ed. J. Shawcross (Oxford, 1907), 2 Vols.

The Collected Letters of S. T. Coleridge, ed. E. L. Griggs (Oxford, 1956–9), Vols. I–IV.

The Complete Poetical Works, ed. E. H. Coleridge (Oxford, 1912), 2 Vols.

The Friend, 1818 edition, York Library reprint (1904).

The Notebooks of Samuel Taylor Coleridge, ed. K. Coburn (1957–62), Vols. 1 and 2, Text and Notes.

Further Letters of Gerard Manley Hopkins, ed. Claude C. Abbott (Second edition, 1956).

Poems and Prose of Gerard Manley Hopkins, selected with an Introduction by W. H. Gardner (Penguin Books, Harmondsworth, 1953).

The Correspondence of Gerard Manley Hopkins and Richard Watson Dixon, ed. Claude C. Abbott (1935).

The Journals and Papers of Gerard Manley Hopkins, ed. H. House and G. Storey (1959).

The Letters of Gerard Manley Hopkins to Robert Bridges, ed. Claude C. Abbott (1935).

The Poems of Gerard Manley Hopkins, ed. W. H. Gardner and N. H. Mackenzie (Fourth edition, 1967).

The Sermons and Devotional Writings of Gerard Manley Hopkins, ed. C. Devlin SJ (1959).

Modern Painters (Orpington, 1888), 5 Vols. and Index.

Praeterita, Introduction by Kenneth Clark (1949).

Ruskin as Literary Critic: Selections, ed. A. H. R. Ball (Cambridge, 1928).

Ruskin Today, chosen and annotated by Kenneth Clark (1964).

The Diaries of John Ruskin, ed. J. Evans and J. H. Waterhouse (Oxford, 1956–9), 3 Vols.

The Literary Criticism of John Ruskin, selected, edited and with an Introduction by H. Bloom, Anchor Books (New York, 1965).

The Works of John Ruskin, ed. E. T. Cook and A. Wedderburn (1903–12), 39 Vols.

Journals of Dorothy Wordsworth, ed. E. de Selincourt (1959), 2 Vols.

Wordsworth, William, *A Guide through the District of the Lakes in the North of England*, with an Introduction by W. M. Merchant and illustrated by John Piper (1951).

II. BIOGRAPHICAL AND CRITICAL STUDIES

Abrams, M. H. *The Mirror and the Lamp* (1953; Norton Library paperback, New York, 1958).

Alexander, E. 'Ruskin and Science', *Modern Language Review*, lxiv (1969), pp. 508–21.

Beach, J. W. *The Concept of Nature in Nineteenth Century English Poetry* (1936).

Burd, Van Akin. 'Another Light on the Writing of *Modern Painters*', *PMLA*, lxviii (1953), pp. 755–63.

Cook, E. T. *The Life of John Ruskin* (1912), 2 Vols.

Gardner, W. H. *Gerard Manley Hopkins: A Study of Poetic Idiosyncrasy in Relation to Poetic Tradition* (1944–9), 2 Vols.

Goetz, Mary D. *A Study of Ruskin's Concept of the Imagination* (Washington, 1947).

House, Humphrey. *Coleridge* (1953).

James, D. G. *Scepticism and Poetry: an Essay on the Poetic Imagination* (1937).

Jump, J. D. 'Ruskin's Reputation in the Eighteen-Fifties: the Evidence of the Three Principal Weeklies', *PMLA*, lxiii (1948), pp. 678–85.

Kenyon Critics, The. *Gerard Manley Hopkins* (Connecticut, 1945).

Ladd, Henry. *The Victorian Morality of Art* (New York, 1932).

Levi, Olma C. 'Ruskin's Views on Poetry', *Sewanee Review*, xxxi (1923), pp. 426–45.

Logan, James V. 'Wordsworth and the Pathetic Fallacy', *Modern Language Notes*, lv (1940), pp. 187–91.

Lowes, J. Livingston. *The Road to Xanadu* (1931).

Miles, Josephine. *Pathetic Fallacy in the Nineteenth Century* (California, 1942; Octagon Books, New York, 1965).

Moorman, Mary. *William Wordsworth, A Biography* (Oxford, 1957–65; Oxford paperback, 1968), 2 Vols.

Noel, Roden. 'On the Use of Metaphor and Pathetic Fallacy in Poetry', *Fortnightly Review*, v (1866), pp. 670–84.

Rosenberg, J. D. *The Darkening Glass. A Portrait of Ruskin's Genius* (1963).

Sambrook, J. *A Poet Hidden. The Life of Richard Watson Dixon* (1962).

Townsend, F. G. *Ruskin and the Landscape Feeling, Illinois Studies in Language and Literature*, xxxv, no. 3 (1951).

Warren, A. H. *English Poetic Theory, 1825–65* (Princeton, 1950).

Wellek, R. *A History of Modern Criticism, 1750–1950* (1955–66), Vols. 1–3.

NOTES

INTRODUCTION

1 Josephine Miles, *Pathetic Fallacy in the Nineteenth Century* (1942), p. 88.
2 ibid., pp. 108–9. Miss Miles's study of the fallacy is an important exception to current indifference. She confines her attention to 'detailed observation' (p. 4) of literary phraseology, but I am indebted to her discussion of 'the problem of relation between self and object' (p. 6).
3 ibid., p. 6.

I. COLERIDGE AND THE WORLD OF SENSE

1 *Biographia Literaria and Aesthetical Essays*, ed. J. Shawcross (1907), i, 174. Referred to as Shawcross.
2 Shawcross, i, 202.
3 Introduction, i, p. li.
4 Ch. xv, section 3; Shawcross, ii, 16–18.
5 Shawcross, ii, 253.
6 ibid., p. 259.
7 *The Friend*, Essay VI, Second Section; 1818 edition (reprinted 1904), pp. 332–3.
8 ibid., p. 333.
9 'On Poesy or Art'; Shawcross, ii, 258.
10 (1953) pp. 292–3; and see whole section, 'Wordsworth and Coleridge on Personification and Myth', pp. 290–7.
11 First published anonymously as an introduction to Joseph Wilkinson's collection of Lake District prints, and as a separate signed volume in 1822. See M. Moorman, *William Wordsworth, A Biography* (1957–65), ii, 157–64 and 384, note 1. See also p. 53 below.
12 1951 edition, with illustrations by John Piper, p. 23. Quotations are all taken from this edition. Referred to as *Guide*.
13 *Guide*, p. 55.
14 ibid., p. 35.
15 ibid., p. 55.
16 ibid., p. 70.
17 ibid., p. 63.
18 ibid., pp. 81–2.
19 ibid., p. 83. There is also the evidence given by W. J. B. Owen that Wordsworth wrote an essay on the Sublime and the Beautiful, 'designed at one stage as an introduction to his *Guide to the Lakes* and which is based mainly on the mind's reaction to the mountainous scenery of the Lake District.' (*Wordsworth as Critic*, Toronto, 1969, pp. 203–4.)
20 *Guide*, Introduction, p. 26.
21 ibid., pp. 73–6.
22 *Journals of Dorothy Wordsworth*, ed. E. de Selincourt (1959), i, 321. Referred to as *DWJ*.

23 29 and 30 August 1800; *DWJ*, i, 57.
24 16 May 1800; *DWJ*, i, 38.
25 20 October 1800; *DWJ*, i, 68.
26 13 April 1802; *DWJ*, i, 130.
27 31 October 1800; *DWJ*, i, 70.
28 12 December 1801; *DWJ*, i, 90.
29 23 April 1802; *DWJ*, i, 137.
30 *DWJ*, i, 82.
31 'Recollections of a Tour Made in Scotland, 1803'; *DWJ*, i, 276–7.
32 1 March 1798; *DWJ*, i, 11.
33 30 October 1802; *DWJ*, i, 184.
34 'Excursion on the Banks of Ullswater, November 1805'; *DWJ*, i, 414–15.
35 *DWJ*, i, 239.
36 *DWJ*, i, 286.
37 *The Notebooks of S. T. Coleridge*, ed. K. Coburn (1957–62), Volumes 1 and 2, Text and Notes. References given indicate volume, followed by entry number. The letter 'n' refers to volume containing editor's notes.
38 e.g., 'O for Sir G.B. to give permanence to these superlative Masses of Clouds over the Convoy'; Malta voyage, 1804 (2.2008).
39 Shawcross, i, 129.
40 *Coleridge* (1953), p. 48.
41 Letter to Cottle, 3 July 1797; *Collected Letters of S. T. Coleridge*, ed. E. L. Griggs (1956–9), i, 330–1.
42 *Coleridge*, p. 53.
43 16 October 1797; Griggs, i, 210.
44 See p. 9.
45 See J. Livingston Lowes, *The Road to Xanadu* (1931), p. 39 and p. 474, note 2. Other scientific works the Notebooks suggest knowledge of include Richard Kirwan's *Elements of Mineralogy* (1794) and Priestley's *Experiments and Observations on Different Kinds of Air* (1774–86). Coleridge's notes on Humphry Davy's lectures on Gases in January/February 1802 show that his painter's eye as well as his scientific mind was pleased by the experiments: 'Sulphur . . . heated . . . in Oxygen Gas a most beautiful purple' (1.1098).
46 *Coleridge*, p. 54.
47 1.218–22, and notes.
48 Shawcross, ii, 254.
49 There is a rather confused attempt in the poem to translate the 'green mountain' into an allegorical 'Hill of Knowledge' (49–50), a point which supports the close identification in Coleridge's mind of topographical with intellectual experience.
50 In a quarto pamphlet, 1798; see E. H. Coleridge, *Complete Poetical Works* (1912), i, 240–1.

2. RUSKIN AND 'THE PURE FACT'

1 *Praeterita*, Introduction by Kenneth Clark (1949), pp. 131, 175.
2 E. T. Cook, *The Life of John Ruskin* (1912), i, 97. Referred to as Cook.
3 *The Works of John Ruskin*, ed. E. T. Cook and A. Wedderburn (1903–12), ii, xxvii. Referred to as *Works*.
4 *Works*, ii, xxx.
5 op. cit., p. 84.
6 ibid., p. 34.

7 ibid., p. 28.
8 ibid., p. 93.
9 ibid., p. 42.
10 ibid., p. 156.
11 *The Diaries of John Ruskin*, ed. Joan Evans and J. H. Waterhouse (1956–9), i, 247. Referred to as *Diaries*.
12 *Works*, i, xlvi.
13 *Works*, i, 194.
14 *Guide*, Introduction, p. 32.
15 *The Victorian Morality of Art* (1932), pp. 61, 153f.
16 See p. 73.
17 Statement made as background information to exhibition *Englishmen in Italy*, water-colours and drawings of Italian scenes by English artists, Victoria and Albert Museum, 1968.
18 op. cit., p. 53.
19 *Praeterita*, pp. 141–2.
20 ibid., pp. 47–8.
21 *Diaries*, i, 74.
22 *Modern Painters*, ii, Epilogue (1883) §3. Referred to as *MP*, with volume, part, section, chapter and paragraph numbers as appropriate.
23 *Praeterita*, p. 268.
24 ibid., p. 281.
25 ibid., p. 285.
26 'Another Light on the Writing of Modern Painters', *PMLA* lxviii (1953), 755–63.
27 *Praeterita*, p. 298.
28 Cook, i, 130.
29 *Praeterita*, p. 205.
30 *MP* III, ch. xii §8.
31 Shawcross, ii, 90–1.
32 Cook, i, 48–9.
33 17 January; *Diaries*, i, 143.
34 27 January; *Diaries*, i, 146.
35 6 January; *Diaries*, i, 136.
36 *Diaries*, i, 186.
37 2 January; *Diaries*, i, 132.
38 1 May; *Diaries*, i, 180.
39 8 May; *Diaries*, i, 185.
40 Quoted in Catalogue to Royal Academy of Arts Bicentenary Exhibition, 1968, pp. 84 and 86.
41 13 May 1843; *Diaries*, i, 246.
42 Introduction to *MP*, *Works*, iii, p. xxxiii.
43 Cook, i, 128.
44 *MP* II, Epilogue §3.
45 *English Poetic Theory, 1825–1865* (1950), p. 12.
46 ibid., p. 179.
47 *MP* I, Preface to Second Edition §46.
48 27 September; *Diaries*, ii, 511.
49 28 September; *Diaries*, ii, 524.
50 *MP* I, Preface to Second Edition §39.
51 *MP* I, ibid. §§21–33.
52 *MP* I, Part II, Section I, ch. ii §§1–2.

53 *MP* I, Part II, Section VI, ch. iii §6.
54 *MP* I, Part II, Section III, ch. iii §6.
55 *MP* I, Part II, Section II, ch. ii §15.
56 *MP* I, Part II, Section IV, ch. i §6.
57 *MP* I, Part II, Section III, ch. iv §14.
58 *MP* V, Part VI, ch. vi §11.
59 *MP* III, ch. xvii §43.
60 *MP* III, ch. x §5.
61 Cook, i, 140.
62 *MP* I, Part II, Section I, ch. vii §46.
63 *MP* IV, ch. xiv §18.
64 *MP* IV, ch. xviii §7.
65 *MP* IV, ch. xvii §37.
66 *MP* I, Part II, Section IV, ch. iv §§13, 28.
67 *MP* I, Part II, Section IV, ch. iii §13.
68 *MP* IV, ch. xv §24.
69 *MP* I, Part II, Section V, ch. iii §24.
70 *Victorian Morality of Art*, p. 209.
71 *MP* I, Part II, Section VI, ch. i §14.
72 *MP* V, Part VI, ch. vii §12.
73 *MP* V, Part VI, ch. v §1.
74 *MP* V, Part VI, ch. viii §5.
75 *MP* I, Part II, Section I, ch. vi §1.
76 *MP* I, Part II, Section V, ch. i §1.
77 *MP* I, Part II, Section I, ch. vi §1.
78 *MP* I, Part II, Section IV, ch. iii §4.
79 *MP* IV, ch. xv §11.
80 *MP* I, Part II, Section II, ch. ii §15, ch. iii §6.
81 *MP* IV, ch. iv §4. The sentence is printed in capitals.
82 *MP* I, Part II, Section I, ch. ii §7.
83 *MP* II, Section II, ch. iv §7; for Ruskin's discussion of the imagination, see *MP* II, Section II, *passim.*
84 *The Stones of Venice*, Vol. III, ch. ii §10.
85 *MP* V, Part IX, ch. i §§8–9.
86 *MP* III, ch. xvii §31.
87 *MP* III, ch. xvi §16.
88 *MP* I, Part II, Section IV, ch. ii §21.
89 *MP* III, ch. xvii §32.
90 *MP* V, Epilogue.
91 *MP* I, Part II, Section VI, ch. iii §24.
92 Kenneth Clark, *Ruskin Today* (1964), p. 85.
93 *MP* II, Epilogue (1883) §7.
94 *MP* IV, ch. xx §43.
95 *Victorian Morality of Art*, p. 189.
96 ibid., pp. 149–59, 371 note 18.
97 *MP* V, Part VII, ch. iv §23.
98 p. 205.
99 *MP* III, ch. xii, ch. xiii §§1–3.
100 *Works*, v, 201, note.
101 A. H. Ball, *Ruskin as Literary Critic* (1928), Introduction, p. 22.
102 *MP* III, ch. i §13.
103 J. V. Logan, 'Wordsworth and the Pathetic Fallacy', *MLN*, lv (1940), 190.

104 *Ruskin and the Landscape Feeling* (1951), p. 55, note.
105 *MP* III, ch. xvii §§3–6.
106 Ladd, op. cit., p. 142.
107 *MP* III, ch. xvi §28.
108 *MP* III, ch. xvi §38.
109 *MP* III, ch. xvi §37.
110 *MP* III, ch. xvi §29.
111 Quoted from *The Spectator*, 2 February 1856; J. D. Jump, 'Ruskin's Reputation in the Eighteen-Fifties: the Evidence of the Three Principal Weeklies', *PMLA*, lxiii (1948), 679.
112 Cook, i, 143–5.
113 Clark, *Ruskin Today*, p. 86.
114 Cook, ii, 572.
115 pp. 340–1.
116 *MP* V, Epilogue.
117 2 September 1835; *Diaries*, i, 58–9.
118 9 June 1841; *Diaries*, i, 200–1.
119 *Diaries*, i, 269.
120 *DWJ*, ii, 88–90.
121 *MP* I, Part II, Section v, ch. ii §2.
122 See *Poetical Works*, i, 376–7, and Moorman, *William Wordsworth*, i, 577.
123 *Diaries*, i, 294.
124 p. 300.
125 Quoted Cook, i, 116.
126 *Works*, xvi, 269–70.
127 *Diaries*, i, 294.
128 i, 115.
129 4 November 1840; *Diaries*, i, 103.
130 *MP* V, Part VII, ch. iv §6.
131 *MP* I, Part II, Section III, ch. iv §23.
132 *MP* I, Part II, Section III, ch. ii §14, ch. iii §§20, 32.
133 Letter to Harrison, 1841; quoted Cook, i, 115.
134 *MP* I, Part II, Section v, ch. iii §§23–4.
135 *Praeterita*, pp. 296–7.
136 *MP* I, Part II, Section v, ch. iii §30.
137 *MP* I, Part II, Section IV, ch. ii §19.
138 p. 397.
139 p. 398.
140 *Works*, xv, 97.
141 *MP* IV, ch. xi §11.
142 *MP* IV, ch. xviii §11.
143 *MP* I, Part II, Section III, ch. iii §17.
144 *MP* I, Part II, Section III, ch. iv §19.
145 *MP* I, Part II, Section v, ch. iii §12.
146 *MP* IV, ch. vii §2.
147 *Diaries*, ii, 370–1.
148 *MP* IV, ch. xiv §18.
149 *The Elements of Drawing*; *Works*, xv, 116.
150 *MP* I, Part II, Section VI, ch. i §14.
151 *MP* I, Part II, Section VI, ch. i §23.
152 *MP* V, Part VI, ch. viii §4.
153 p. xvi.

154 *The Elements of Drawing*; *Works*, xv, 74.
155 *MP* V, Part vi, ch. x §10.
156 14 July 1835; *Diaries*, i, 21.
157 *Praeterita*, p. 483.
158 *MP* I, Part ii, Section iii, ch. ii §5.
159 *MP* I, Part ii, Section iii, ch. ii §6.
160 14 July 1835; *Diaries*, i, 22.
161 *MP* V, Part vii, ch. iii §13.
162 19 June 1849; *Diaries*, ii, 391–2.
163 *MP* I, Part ii, Section iii, ch. iv §24.
164 *MP* V, Part vii, ch. ii §18.
165 17 May; *Diaries*, ii, 514.
166 *MP* V, Part ix, ch. ix §§3–5.
167 A. H. Warren, *English Poetic Theory*, p. 20.
168 *MP* II, Section i, ch. xiii §§13, 1.
169 *MP* I, Part ii, Section iv, ch. iv §15.
170 *Deucalion*; *Works*, xxvi, 334.
171 *MP* V, Part vi, chs. i–iii.
172 *MP* I, Part ii, Section iv, ch. iv §30.
173 *MP* V, Epilogue.

3. HOPKINS AND 'THE SWEET ESPECIAL SCENE'

1 22 June 1879; *Letters of G. M. Hopkins to Robert Bridges*, ed. Claude C. Abbott (1935), p. 84. Referred to as *Letters to Bridges*.
2 10 March 1879; *Correspondence of G. M. Hopkins and R. W. Dixon*, ed. Claude C. Abbott (1935), p. 20. Referred to as *Dixon Corr.*
3 6 April 1881, 16 September 1881, 26 September 1881; ibid., pp. 48, 56, 64.
4 J. Sambrook, *A Poet Hidden* (1962), p. 50.
5 Notes on the Spiritual Exercises; *The Sermons and Devotional Writings of G. M. Hopkins*, ed. C. Devlin sj (1959), p. 122. Referred to as Devlin.
6 Devlin, p. 123.
7 26 May 1879; *Letters to Bridges*, p. 83.
8 *The Journals and Papers of G. M. Hopkins*, ed. H. House and G. Storey (1959), p. 127. Referred to as *JP*.
9 Preface, *JP*, p. xxiii.
10 *JP*, p. 128.
11 W. H. Gardner, *Poems and Prose of G. M. Hopkins* (1953), Introduction, p. xx.
12 See p. 120.
13 8 April 1873; *JP*, p. 230.
14 c. 14 March 1871; *JP*, p. 205.
15 24 February 1873; *JP*, p. 230.
16 13 June 1871; *JP*, p. 211.
17 *JP*, p. 211.
18 *Poems and Prose of G. M. Hopkins*, p. xxi.
19 Introduction to Spiritual Writings; Devlin, p. 109.
20 Note 138; Devlin, p. 290.
21 Devlin, p. 109.
22 Devlin, p. 239.
23 'Scotus and Hopkins'; Devlin, Appendix ii, p. 351.
24 1870; *JP*, p. 199.
25 15 February 1879; *Letters to Bridges*, p. 66.

26 17 August 1874; *JP*, p. 254.
27 'Parmenides'; *JP*, p. 129.
28 Also in the 'Platonic Dialogue', 'On the Origin of Beauty', 1865.
29 'Poetic Diction'; *JP*, p. 85.
30 ibid; *JP*, p. 84.
31 'Poetry and Verse'; *JP*, p. 289.
32 'Poetic Diction'; *JP*, p. 84.
33 'On the Origin of Beauty'; *JP*, p. 114.
34 Notes: 9 February 1868; *JP*, p. 126.
35 'The Origin of our Moral Ideas'; *JP*, p. 83.
36 Notes: 9 February 1868; *JP*, p. 126.
37 *Dixon Corr.*, Appendix II, pp. 161–6. The letters appear in the issues of 16 November 1882, 15 November 1883, and 3 January 1884.
38 30 October 1884; *Nature*, xxx (1884), 633. The letter is signed 'G.M.H. Dublin'. For full text, see Appendix, p. 148.
39 *Dixon Corr.*, Appendix II, op. cit., p. 165.
40 ibid., p. 163.
41 *Dixon Corr.*, *Nature*, xxx (1884), 633; and see Appendix, p. 149.
42 Appendix II, p. 164.
43 See Preface, *JP*, p. xxx, and H. House, *Coleridge*, p. 10.
44 c. 10 March 1868; *JP*, p. 162.
45 3 August 1868; *JP*, p. 185.
46 28 March 1868; *JP*, p. 163.
47 12 February 1870; *JP*, p. 196.
48 Winter 1870; *JP*, p. 201.
49 29 April 1871; *JP*, p. 208.
50 Early Diaries, 1863; *JP*, p. 8.
51 *Notebooks*, 1.1589; quoted *JP*, p. 442.
52 8 November 1874; *JP*, p. 261.
53 27 April 1871; *JP*, p. 207.
54 *JP*, p. 201.
55 *JP*, pp. 203–4.
56 19 July 1866; *JP*, p. 146.
57 6 April 1868; *JP*, p. 163.
58 *Gerard Manley Hopkins: a Study of Poetic Idiosyncrasy in Relation to Poetic Tradition* (1944–9), i, 11.
59 To A. W. M. Baillie, 10 July 1863; *Further Letters of G. M. Hopkins*, ed. Claude C. Abbott (1956), p. 202.
60 'Hopkins's Drawings'; Appendix I, *JP*, p. 455.
61 11 August 1880; *Diaries*, iii, 981.
62 23 July 1874; *JP*, p. 249.
63 9 August 1873; *JP*, p. 234.
64 ibid.
65 16 August 1873; *JP*, p. 235.
66 10 August 1872; *JP*, p. 223.
67 *JP*, p. 184.
68 10 August 1872; *JP*, p. 223.
69 13 August 1874; *JP*, p. 251.
70 1865; *JP*, p. 66.
71 9 May 1871; *JP*, p. 208.
72 1873; *JP*, p. 240.
73 5 November 1880; *Diaries*, iii, 992–3.

74 14 August 1872; *JP*, p. 224.
75 22 August 1867, entry added 'for July 6, 1866'; *JP*, p. 152.
76 'End of March and beginning of April' 1871; *JP*, pp. 205–6.
77 *JP*, pp. 144–5.
78 19 July 1866; *JP*, p. 146.
79 9/11 May 1871; *JP*, p. 209.
80 May and June 1874; *JP*, pp. 245–7.
81 He does not, however, confuse literal copyist work with true artistic seeing, any more than Ruskin does. Of Holman Hunt's 'Shadow of Death', he says, 'No inscape of composition whatever—not known and if it had been known it could scarcely bear up against such realism'; *JP*, p. 248.
82 'Hopkins's Drawings'; Appendix I, *JP*, p. 454.
83 *JP*, p. 134.
84 28 July 1868; *JP*, p. 183.
85 13 July 1868; *JP*, p. 173.
86 19 July 1868; *JP*, p. 178.
87 20 July 1868; *JP*, p. 178.
88 15 July 1868; *JP*, p. 174.
89 16 July 1868; *JP*, p. 175.
90 Early Diaries, 1863; *JP*, pp. 5, 11.
91 'Philological Notes'; Appendix III, *JP*, p. 499.
92 Early Diaries, 1864; *JP*, pp. 46–7.
93 *MP* II, Section I, ch. xiii §1.
94 Devlin, p. 239.
95 ibid.
96 *MP* II, Section I, ch. iii §16.
97 Devlin, p. 239.
98 *MP* II, Section I, ch. iii §16.
99 *MP* V, Part VII, ch. i §9.
100 *Works*, xv, 130.
101 13 September 1875; *Diaries*, iii, 861.
102 *MP* I, Part II, Section III, ch. iii §21.
103 *MP* V, Part VII, ch. iv §5.
104 *MP* I, Part II, Section IV, ch. i §3.
105 *MP* V, Epilogue (1888).
106 *MP* I. Part II, Section III. ch. iv §§30–4.

INDEX

Abrams, M. H., 9–10
Athenaeum, The, 61

Baillie, A. W. M., 159
Ball, A. H., 76, 156
Bartram, William, 33
Beaumont, Sir George, 19, 20, 154
Blackwood's Edinburgh Magazine, 59
Bowles, Rev. W. L., 20
Bridges, Robert, 103, 105, 158
Brontë, Charlotte, 81
Browning, Elizabeth, 81
Browning, Robert, 81, 104
Brun, Friederika
  Ode to Chamouni, 86
Buckland, William, 53, 73
Burd, Van Akin, 56–7
Byron, Lord, 48, 51
  Childe Harold, 54
  Don Juan, 54
  Manfred, 54, 58

Christ, Jesus, 110–11, 136, 140, 141,
  145–6
Clark, Lord, 81, 98, 154, 156, 157
Coburn, Kathleen, 19, 22, 23, 27,
  29, 30, 154
Coleridge, Ernest Hartley, 115
Coleridge, Hartley, 43, 44, 45
Coleridge, Samuel Taylor, 1–3, 5–
  47, 48, 49, 55, 66–7, 71, 72, 73,
  75, 77, 82, 83, 99, 102, 111, 114,
  116–19, 132, 140, 146, 153–4
  Poems
  Dejection: an Ode, 46, 47
  Fears in Solitude, 35–7, 38, 67
  Frost at Midnight, 1, 33, 38, 42–4,
    45, 102

Hymn before Sunrise in the Vale of
  Chamouni, 83, 86–7
Kubla Khan, 34–5, 40
Ode to the Departing Year, 30
Reflections on Having Left a Place of
  Retirement, 35–6, 37
The Ancient Mariner, 35
The Brook, 21
The Nightingale, 38, 40, 44–6
This Lime-Tree Bower my Prison, 38,
  40–2, 45
To a Young Friend, 39–40, 45
Prose
Biographia Literaria, 3–10, 11, 21,
  46, 59, 62, 67, 75, 153
Letters, 20, 28, 154
Notebooks, 2, 15, 18–34, 35, 39,
  40, 42, 46–7, 55, 115–18, 140,
  146, 154, 159
'On Poesy or Art', 8, 9, 37, 47,
  153
The Friend, 9, 28, 153
Coleridge, Sara, 80
Cook, E. T., 52, 65, 89, 154, 155,
  156, 157
Cottle, Joseph, 154

Dante Alighieri, 76, 77
Darwin, Erasmus, 34
Davy, Sir Humphry, 9, 10, 154
De Quincey, Thomas, 75
Devlin, Christopher, 110, 111, 117,
  158, 160
Dixon, Richard, 103–4, 115, 158,
  159
  Fallen Rain, 103
Domecq, Adèle, 48, 54
Duns Scotus, 105, 110, 158

Friendship's Offering, 48, 52

Gardner, W. H., 107, 109, 119–20, 158

Harrison, W. H., 57, 157
Homer, 77
Hopkins, Gerard Manley, 1–3, 79, 80, 102, 103–50, 158–60
Poems
'As kingfishers catch fire', 135–6, 146
Binsey Poplars, 107, 133–4
God's Grandeur, 140, 143–4
Henry Purcell, 103, 105
Hurrahing in Harvest, 137–8, 142, 145
Ribblesdale, 142
Spelt from Sibyl's Leaves, 140, 141
Spring, 140, 141, 143
'Terrible sonnets', 133
That Nature is a Heraclitean Fire, 138, 140
The May Magnificat, 140
The Sea and the Skylark, 140, 141
The Starlight Night, 1, 132, 143
The Windhover, 139–40, 141, 143, 146
The Wreck of the Deutschland, 132–3
To What Serves Mortal Beauty?, 147
Prose
Devotional Writings, 104–5, 110–111, 158, 160
Journals, 104, 107, 108, 111, 115, 116–32, 136, 137, 140, 158–60
Letters, 103–4, 105, 120, 158, 159
Letters to *Nature*, 115–16, 124, 130, 148–50, 159
Notes, 112–14, 159
'On the Origin of Beauty', 113, 159
'Parmenides', 106, 159
'Poetic Diction', 112–14, 159
'Poetry and Verse', 112–14, 159
'The Origin of our Moral Ideas', 113, 159
House, Humphrey, 21, 26, 33, 117, 158, 159

Hunt, Holman, 160

'Joyce's Scientific Dialogues', 54
Jump, J. D., 157

Keats, John, 132
Kirwan, Richard, 154

Ladd, Henry, 53, 54, 67, 72, 78, 157
Logan, J. V., 77, 156
Loudon's *Magazine of Natural History*, 52, 53
Lowes, J. Livingston, 154

Merchant, W. M., 11, 53
Miles, Josephine, 1, 2, 153
Moorman, Mary, 153, 157

Nature, 115–16, 148, 159

Owen, W. J. B., 153

Parmenides, 106, 159
Piper, John, 120, 129, 153
Poole, Thomas, 28
Priestley, Joseph, 29, 154
Purcell, Henry, 103, 105

Royal Academy, The, 59, 61, 129, 155
Ruskin, John, 1–3, 45, 48–102, 103–114, 115, 116, 119–21, 123, 124–5, 126, 127–9, 130, 131, 132, 133, 134–47, 154–8, 160
Poems
Account of a Tour on the Continent, 50
A Tour through France to Chamouni, 51
A Walk in Chamouni, 49
Glenfarg, 50
Iteriad, 50
Mont Blanc Revisited, 49
On the Appearance of a Sudden Cloud of Yellow Fog Covering Everything with Darkness, 50
The Arve at Cluse, 49
The Grave of the Poet, 50

Verse Letter to John James Ruskin, 50
Prose
Deucalion, 100, 141, 158
Diaries, 2, 52, 54, 57, 60–1, 63, 82–3, 87–9, 96, 99, 120, 131, 138–9, 155, 157, 158, 159, 160
'Enquiries on the Cause of the Colour of the Water of the Rhine', 52
'Facts and Considerations on the Strata of Mont Blanc; and on some Instances of twisted Strata observable in Switzerland', 52
Letters, 57–8, 157
Modern Painters, 1, 2, 3, 48, 52, 55–56, 57, 58, 59–102, 103, 104, 115, 125, 128, 131, 136–7, 140, 141–2, 144–7, 155–8, 160
Praeterita, 51–2, 56–7, 58, 75, 81, 88, 94, 98, 154, 155, 157, 158
The Elements of Drawing, 94–5, 125, 129, 137, 157, 158
The Stones of Venice, 70, 81, 156
The Two Paths, 88
Ruskin, John James, 48, 50
Ruysdael, Jakob van, 86

Sambrook, J., 104, 158
Scott, Sir Walter, 50, 79–80
Sedgwick, Adam, 53, 73
Shakespeare, William, 6, 7, 8, 9, 10, 26
  King Lear, 7
  Othello, 7
Shawcross, J., 6, 153, 154, 155
Shelley, Percy Bysshe, 75
Spectator, The, 157

Storey, Graham, 106, 117, 158

Tennyson, Alfred Lord, 79, 81
Times, The, 61
Townsend, F., 77
Turner, J. M. W., 3, 23, 58, 59–65, 68, 71, 74, 75, 80, 86, 88–9, 90–1, 95, 99, 124, 129, 144

Victoria and Albert Museum, The, 155

Ward, Alan, 131
Warren, A. H., 62, 158
Wedderburn, A., 52, 154
Wilkinson, Joseph, 153
Wordsworth, Dorothy, 2, 11, 15, 18, 20, 21–2, 25, 26, 29, 32, 34, 40, 82, 99, 140, 153–4
  'Excursion on the Banks of Ullswater, November 1805', 11, 154
  Journals (Alfoxden and Grasmere), 11, 15–17, 154
  Journal of a Tour on the Continent, 83–4, 85, 157
  'Recollections of a Tour made in Scotland, 1803', 11, 15, 16–18, 22, 154
Wordsworth, Mary, 16
Wordsworth, William, 3, 7, 9, 10, 11, 16, 17, 18, 20, 25, 26, 29, 32, 34, 53, 57, 59, 71, 73, 75, 77, 79, 80, 132, 140, 153
  A Guide through the District of the Lakes, 11–15, 34, 53, 153, 155
  Lines composed a few Miles above Tintern Abbey, 12–13
  The Excursion, 71